anatomy of
contemporary
furniture

john g. shea

anatomy of
contemporary
furniture

VAN NOSTRAND REINHOLD COMPANY
New York, Cincinnati, Toronto, London, Melbourne

Van Nostrand Reinhold Company Regional Offices:
New York   Cincinnati   Chicago   Millbrae   Dallas

Van Nostrand Reinhold Company International Offices:
London . Toronto   Melbourne

Copyright © 1965, 1973 by Litton Educational Publishing, Inc.
Library of Congress Catalog Card Number 73-6684
ISBN 0-442-27543-9

First published in 1965 under the title *Contemporary Furniture Making
for Everybody*

Revised edition published in 1973 by
Van Nostrand Reinhold Company
A Division of Litton Educational Publishing, Inc.
450 West 33rd Street, New York, N.Y. 10001

16 15 14 13 12 11 10 9 8 7 6 5 4 3 2 1

preface

During the few years which have elapsed since the original edition of this book was first published, many changes have evolved in the furnishing of our homes. In the past, a distinct line of demarcation existed between *"modern"* and *"traditional"* furniture forms. People liked one style or the other—*but not both.*

Now, however, the newer furniture designs seem to have gained more popular acceptance. The reason for this is obvious: Every period of history produced its own designs—and the current contemporary style simply reflects the natural expression of today.

Even the most ardent traditionalists would not be content to depend on candles and kerosene lamps for illuminating today's homes—nor, would they willingly part with functional appliances which are so essential to our modern way of living. By the same token, the scientific development of contemporary furniture also introduces new functional concepts of convenience and comfort.

So, contemporary furniture has become part of our lives—and it offers many practical advantages: It is of simple organic design, devoid of superfluous embellishment and impractical ornamentation. It blends with other types of functional furniture and melts into the decor of tastefully appointed rooms. It is designed to serve with maximum efficiency. And it complements recent trends toward *mixed-period* furniture combinations.

Actually, there is a strong affinity between the philosophy of contemporary design and that of some traditional furniture forms. This is remarkably evident in the case of *Shaker* furniture, first produced in this country almost two hundred years ago. Shaker craftsmen were the first functionalists. Their furniture designs, governed by religious edicts, disdained superfluous weight and ornamentation which did not contribute to functional qualifications. Their doctrine of design was aptly expressed by their Elders: *"That which has in itself the highest use possesses the greatest beauty."* The same doctrine is scrupulously adhered to by leading contemporary designers today.

In this book we endeavor to present a fair cross section of typical contemporary furniture designs—and also show how this furniture is made. Our primary purpose is to provide readers with a graphic exposition of this furniture in its present stage of development. The intention is *to get at it* in such a way as to enable readers to *look it over—select it—*and *buy it—*with a better understanding of what it has to offer. Specifically, we then try to show *how to work with it—assemble it—install it—*and *create comfortable home environments* with it. Also, with the accompanying do-it-yourself instructions and plans, we hope to encourage practical homemakers to try their hands at making their own contemporary furniture.

Because of its simplicity of construction, contemporary furniture is easy to build. While these designs are constructed in conformance with functional "contemporary" principles, for the most part they may be regarded as just plain practical.

As an added assist to the do-it-yourselfer, it will be observed that much of this furniture is assembled of stock hardware and prefabricated parts. Boards, cut to required lengths, are attached to metal brackets to make convenient shelves. Wall standards and tension poles support shelving and cabinets to create a variety of practical and decorative effects. Separate, attachable legs and metal pedestals, of various types and sizes, facilitate the assembly of functional tables, desks, chairs and benches. Most of this construction can be accomplished with a minimum of tools and skill.

An abundance of photo-sequences are presented throughout the book to demonstrate in step-by-step detail exactly how the various jobs are performed. They show the actual construction of typical contemporary projects with hand and power tools. Also included are visual instructions on assembly of stock parts, kits, installation of sectional components and "how-to" details of covering, upholstering and finishing. Going beyond the actual construction of contemporary furniture, this book also endeavors to explore related aspects of creating decorative room effects with this furniture.

So, the aim of this book is not only to provide better consumer understanding of this dynamic new design development, but also to encourage practical homemakers to create their own contemporary milieu.

Finally, it is hoped that all readers will observe that the mellow contemporary designs of today have acquired significant maturity of form and structure. Unlike the box shapes of preliminary *modern* which appeared several decades ago, many of the designs shown in this book have endured from the first edition to become *classics* in their own time. Some, of course, have succumbed to the constant turnover of manufacturers' production. But this does not detract from the classical distinction of their design.

Greenwich, Connecticut   JOHN G. SHEA
August 2, 1973

acknowledgments

For their courteous cooperation in furnishing illustrations, information and materials, separately identified and credited in this book, the author wishes to thank the following companies and organizations:

Acushnet Process Corporation; American Plywood Association; American Saint Gobain Corporation; Ardor Manufacturing Company; Armstrong Cork Company; Artek, Finland; Barclay Manufacturing Company; Black & Decker Manufacturing Company; Brown-Saltman Corporation; Burgess Vibrocrafters, Inc.; Champion International; E. Kold Christensen, Denmark; Disston Division: H. K. Porter Company; Doo-It Store; Drexel Furniture Company; E. I. du Pont de Nemours & Company; Fine Hardwoods Association; Firestone Tire & Rubber Company; Furn-A-Kit, Inc.; General Foam Corporation; Georgia-Pacific Corporation; Gerber Wrought Iron Products, Inc.; Hardwood Manufacturers, Inc.; Hardwood Plywood Association.

Also, Herman Miller, Inc.; Heywood-Wakefield Company; Hooker Furniture Corporation; Interna, Denmark; Knoll International; Libbey-Owens-Ford Company; Millers Falls Company; National Furniture Manufacturers Association; National Lumber Manufacturers Association; Nicholson File Company; Pittsburgh Plate Glass Company; Reynolds Metals Company; Royal Systems; Southern Furniture Manufacturers Association; Stanley Tools; The Door Store; Tip Top Brush Company, Watco-Dennis Corporation; Western Wood Products Association.

contents

3 HOW TO BUILD CONTEMPORARY FURNITURE STEP-BY-STEP

4 HOW TO CREATE CONTEMPORARY ROOMS

5 CONTEMPORARY CLASSICS

6 CONTEMPORARY BUILT-INS

7 CONTEMPORARY COMPONENTS AND KITS

8 HOW TO COVER & UPHOLSTER CONTEMPORARY FURNITURE

9 CONTEMPORARY FINISHING

10 CONTEMPORARY SOURCES

1

CONTEMPORARY FURNITURE

Designs by Harry Bertoia, courtesy Knoll International

In a world churning with change, where designs and devices become obsolete within a few years after their origin, *furniture* remains uniquely ageless. For many of our homes today are furnished with traditional furniture designs which originated centuries ago.

Thus, unlike other things of modern utility—our automobiles, refrigerators, television sets and washing machines (which seem to be designed with built-in obsolescence to make way for effusions of new yearly models)—good furniture stands inviolate to rapid change. Indeed, the prudent furniture designer realizes this and only the foolhardy dares wander too far afield of traditional forms.

But this does not mean that furniture design has remained oblivious to *improvement*. Each "period" and "style" of furniture has, in fact, displayed its own distinctive characteristics and designers have always been motivated by the desire to create something better—both aesthetically and functionally.

So, in studying the history of furniture, it may be observed that the principal periods and styles are often identified by the names of the designers responsible for their origin. Such names as *Adams, Chippendale, Hepplewhite, Phyfe* and *Sheraton* evoke universal recognition. These men were among the master designers of what we now call "traditional furniture." But one day their accomplishments may be matched with such names as *Aalto, Eames, Nelson, Saarinen, Kjaerholm, Koch,* and many others who are the inspired leaders of contemporary furniture design today.

Prelude to Contemporary Design

Unfortunately, for every inspired furniture designer who has earned a place in the corridors of immortality, dozens of others have fallen by the wayside. These were the imitators and innovators of "new" designs which failed to mature into anything of enduring quality. Only too often the "new" came into being as the flamboyant fad of an era of bad taste.

Just a few decades ago an *avant-garde* of designers assaulted the ramparts of reason to advance their concepts of "modernistic" design. Modernistic furniture was created of cubes. In theory it disdained softness of form and embellishment of any sort. Its dogma could be chanted to the Steinesque lyrics: "*A block is a block is a block.*" Conjuring images of Hitler's Aerie at Berchtesgaden, it produced massive square sofas and chairs drawn up to heavy tables of unadorned box dimensions.

At its best, modernistic furniture was made of fine woods and shiny metals. But as the designs trickled down into mass manufacture, the overbearing proportions were further afflicted with wild "borax" veneers and bent shapes of imponderable purpose.

But even if modernistic design can be credited with nothing else, it did pave the way for creation of a mature and practical *contemporary* style of furniture. Since all things are contemporary to the time of their origin, the designation "Contemporary Furniture" may seem empty and ambiguous. Nevertheless, in accepted usage, it does denote establishment of a stable new style of furniture, not to be confused with experimental styles of "modernistic" and "modern" which preceded its development.

The elegant simplicity of contemporary dining-room furniture is exemplified by the designs pictured above. Chairs by Eero Saarinen; table by Florence Knoll. *Courtesy Knoll International*

Influence of the Industrial Engineer

It was inevitable that the vast social, cultural and scientific changes of the mid-twentieth century would have their effect on the design of furniture as well as all other things. But the creation of a truly "new" style of contemporary furniture seems to have been produced under the influence of modern science as well as artistic aspiration.

Scientific efficiency, in fact, has become the dominating force in development of contemporary design. The insatiable drive of the industrial engineer to obtain greater functional fitness has had its effect in the design of all things, ranging from toothbrushes to skyscrapers. Industrial engineers are dedicated to the proposition that all things can be designed to work better.

One of the first observations of the industrial engineer was that achievement of functional fitness also produced purity of design. A conspicuous example of this is the jet transport aircraft in which myriads of miraculous mechanisms, representing the most sophisticated technical advances, are efficiently housed in a sleek metal vehicle of exquisitely sculptured design. Thus purity of purpose and beauty of design seems to go hand in hand.

While the engineer's criteria of pure "functionalism" was bound to bring about the design of a new style of furniture, the scientific approach had to be "humanized," at least, to the extent of realizing that furniture is a very personal thing and that it must be designed to meet individual tastes.

For the average person, furniture is a long-term investment. It is lived with year in year out during the lifetime of the buyer and often for generations beyond. It becomes part of a person's way of life. We spend approximately *one-third* of our lives lying in beds and, accumulatively, dozens of years more sitting in chairs and

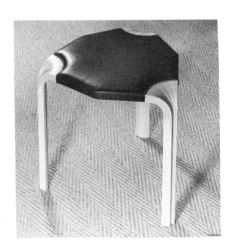

Alvar Aalto of Finland seeks symmetry of bent wood shapes combined with structural glass to create the delicate table design shown above. In the stool, below, the laminated legs seem to flow down from the padded seat. *Courtesy Artek, Finland.*

sofas and eating and working at tables and desks. Thus, since furniture forms such an intimate part of our way of being, its design must reflect our individual needs and tastes as well as embodying sheer scientific functionalism.

The Scandinavian Influence

On basis of the considerations mentioned above, a movement was started in the Scandinavian countries to produce a new style of furniture which combined efficiency of functional fitness with qualifications of human appeal. Variously referred to as "Swedish Modern," "Danish Design," and "Scandinavian Contemporary," much of this furniture, made in Denmark, Finland, Norway, and Sweden, has been imported into this country and has inspired the design of our own contemporary furniture.

While the wide range and diversity of Scandinavian designs defies generalization of description, most of this furniture, as shown on these pages, reflects austere simplicity based on purity of purpose. It eschews pompous ornamentation, depending instead on fine lines, superb craftsmanship and tasteful application of natural materials. It has the fundamental beauty of all things honest unto their purpose.

Simple base construction of table, at top, is accomplished with slim metal brackets which overlap and are joined with screws.

Graceful sweep of folding stool is produced with chromium-plated, twisted steel.

Base brackets of chromium-plated steel support wooden top of this uncomplicated table design.

Steel and bent wood combine to make this attractive side chair. All designs on this page by Poul Kjaerholm. *Courtesy E. Kold Christensen, Denmark.*

5

This room is smartly furnished with modular assembly of sectional wall units. As shown here, this interchangeable wall treatment offers infinite variations of components and arrangements. Each unit is supported with metal brackets attached to wall. Fine wood paneling of background and impeccable construction of units contributes to decorative impact. *Courtesy Royal System.*

Superbly crafted of teak and walnut, these interchangeable furniture units are attached to tension poles to form functional room dividers. The same units may also be fastened to wall standards with ingenious lock-pin devices and metal brackets. Designed by Poul Cadovius and manufactured in Denmark, these fine sectional pieces are imported in the wide variety of designs illustrated in Chapter 7. *Courtesy Royal System.*

The fundamental functional appeal of this metal framed chest becomes amplified when it is joined with matching units to provide multiple drawer space along extended wall areas. It will be noted the ends are made to fit flush to adjoining pieces. While this design is devoid of ornamentation, its fine wood graining provides attractive embellishment. Design by George Nelson.

Courtesy Herman Miller, Inc.

Courtesy Herman Miller, Inc.

Courtesy Knoll International

The Eames chair, above, and the chair of Mies Van Der Rohe, at the right, make use of chromium-plated metal for graceful abbreviation of base structure. Fine styling of these chairs is complemented by their absolute comfort.

Living-room furniture, at bottom right, was designed by Florence Knoll with slim metal bases to create a light and graceful feeling. Designs are distinguished by fine lines and colorful upholstery.

Courtesy Knoll International

Sculptured lines of this chest design are enlivened with caned panel and shaped drawer pulls. Design by Jan Knudsen. *Courtesy Heywood-Wakefield Co.*

Philosophy of Contemporary Design

It is a common misconception that the term "contemporary" represents the extreme opposite of "traditional," when applied to furniture design. Actually, there is not too great a difference between traditional designs of certain fundamental types and some basic contemporary concepts. Certainly the rudimentary, solid wood furniture of early colonial America has much in common with the best contemporary furniture designed today. Both types are essentially functional—and both are devoid of ostentatious ornamentation.

But the line is sharply drawn between contemporary furniture and traditional furniture of the more sophisticated periods. Indeed, the philosophy of contemporary design rules out the use of applied embellishment, elaborately curved and scrolled shapes and decorative turning. It seeks beauty through absolute simplicity.

The effective contemporary designer is constantly concerned with economy of essentials. He must often ask himself: "Is this feature necessary?—And does it contribute anything to the appeal and purpose of the design?"

Obviously, a chair is not made more comfortable by the carving or turning of its legs; nor is a table rendered more serviceable by the amount of decoration it displays. So the contemporary designer discards traditional embellishment insofar as it does not contribute to functional requirements.

Criteria of Serviceability

"That which serves best, looks best," may be the guiding credo of the successful contemporary designer. But since an important aspect of service, as applied to furniture, is the aesthetic fitness of individual designs to live together in close relationship—and thus enhance the livability of their surroundings—the designer must see to it that his end product is, of itself, endowed with beauty. Its beauty, however, may be that of a healthy, well-developed living form rather than an artificial piece of superimposed ornamentation.

Like the efficiency expert who is engaged to detect the "Why?" of all situations which confront him, the contemporary designer is constantly curious about the validity of "accepted" conventions of furniture design. Taking nothing for granted, he approaches each design problem from the standpoint of practicality. Typical of the questions he asks, are the following:

- Are "conventional" sizes and proportions of furniture properly adjusted to the mid-twentieth century home?
- Is it desirable to retain design and construction techniques of centuries ago when newer and more efficient methods and materials are now available?
- Does the furniture design contribute to the ease of housekeeping? Is it easy to clean and maintain? Is it easily moved and rearranged?
- Is the furniture adaptable to specific needs of the individuals who must live with it? Is it suited to average homes with growing children? Can it accommodate family social requirements?
- Is it built sufficiently strong to withstand years of use?
- Does it enhance its environment to produce a pleasing and livable atmosphere?

Eames Chairs

A story is told of two brilliant architectural students, of different nationalities, who met at a Paris design school. Their admiration of each other's work brought them into close friendship. On graduating from the school they promised to keep in touch after they returned to their respective countries.

Several years later they again met at an international convention. After greeting each other warmly, they almost simultaneously inquired:

"What have you been doing since we left school?"

"Well," volunteered one, "I designed several buildings, some skyscrapers, a complex of condominiums, residences for suburban developments, two theaters, a series of shopping centers and . . . But that's enough about *me*. What have *you* been doing over the years?"

"I don't want to brag," replied the other, "but it is just possible that I have developed a design for a perfectly functional *chair!*"

The story may be apocryphal. But in underscoring the formidable and time-consuming feat of designing "*a perfectly functional chair*" it could apply to the work of Charles Eames. For this remarkable architectural designer has become internationally famous for the perfection of his functional chairs. Recognized as "classics" in their own time, Eames chairs touch the lives and seating habits of a preponderant portion of our population. As well as being widely used in homes, both here and abroad, functional seating of Eames design brought new concepts of comfort to the waiting rooms of airports, office buildings and other areas of high-density seating.

The talent of Charles Eames as a furniture designer first came to light when he collaborated with Eero Saarinen to win two awards at the Museum of Modern Art's *Organic Furniture Competition* in 1940-41. Fundamentally, he excelled as an experimenter with new materials and constructional techniques. Early in his career he developed new methods of bending and molding plywood to form the unorthodox shapes of his so-called *potato-chip chair*, shown on the next page. Later, he experimented with metals and plastics to replace the laminated wood shapes of his original designs.

Always, the criterion of comfort has been the hallmark of Eames designs. This he accomplished

Rosewood or walnut veneers, on molded plywood shell, combine with soft leather upholstery and chrome base to make the Eames lounge chair and ottoman about the most comfortable and original seating combination ever designed.

Courtesy Herman Miller, Inc.

The so-called *potato-chip* chair of Eames design started with all parts made of molded plywood. Later the legs and frame were made of chrome steel. The final version, shown above at right, has molded fiberglass seat and back softly laminated with vinyl upholstery.

Because of its adroit adjustment of seat and back contours, Eames' high-backed, swivel-and-tilt chair is exceptionally comfortable. It is also made as an armchair.

through subtle molding of parts to provide restful repose of the human body when placed in seated position. It involved study of the relationship of the body to both the *back* and *seat* of the chair. For Eames observed that in order to be comfortably seated, weight must be supported by both back and buttocks.

Eames was least concerned about how unorthodox his designs might appear as long as they served their functional purpose. His large lounge chair and ottoman looked like something imported from outer space when they first appeared in 1956. But since then they have been acclaimed as a contemporary classic. For as well as being ultra-comfortable, the Eames *"catcher's mit"* lounge chair has become ensconced as a status symbol in tens of thousands of homes, clubs and public buildings.

Perhaps the most important lesson to be learned from Eames designs—as well as those of the other distinguished contemporary designers whose work is shown in this book—is that the superior designs of today may be imbued with all the aesthetic virtue of traditional furniture designs produced centuries ago. These contemporary pieces, of true artistic and functional merit, may endure like their counterparts of yore to represent, in their category, the best cultural expression of our time.

The Eames chaise, below, is as much admired for its sculptural beauty as its obvious comfort.

All photos courtesy Herman Miller, Inc.

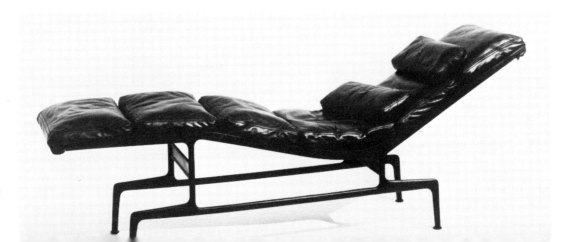

Molded chairs with aluminum bases combine with marble-topped pedestal table to form this graceful group. Designs by Eero Saarinen. *Courtesy Knoll Associates International*

Courtesy Fine Hardwoods Association

Contemporary Materials

Despite scientific advances of other materials, *wood* remains the first choice of the contemporary furniture designer. Because wood is a warm and living material, imbued with its own color and natural characteristics of graining, it is particularly appropriate for the fundamental designs of today. This does not mean, however, that other materials are not used. Indeed, as the illustrations on these pages testify, much contemporary furniture is also constructed wholly or in part of metal, plastics, and glass.

Fine wood graining, as illustrated in panel at right, enriches the surface characteristics of contemporary furniture.

Compartmentation of drawer construction at left, designed by Mogens Koch, shows detailing of fine craftsmanship. *Courtesy Interna, Denmark*

Courtesy Hardwood Manufacturers, Inc.

Courtesy Armstrong Cork Company

Courtesy E. I. du Pont de Nemours & Co.

But for a type of furniture which depends on the inherent appeal of *natural* materials to produce its aesthetic charm, wood, of select species is the obvious choice. Fine, natural, wood graining furnishes surface enrichment so necessary to compensate for the contemporary void of ornate embellishment.

Conspicuous among the "contemporary woods" are such species as teak, walnut, and rosewood. The distinctive color and grain patterns of these woods contribute to the beauty of furniture. Moreover, such woods are easily crafted to the modest shapes of contemporary design.

Oak, the sturdy standby of furniture construction throughout the ages, is again coming back for increased use. The strength and structural characteristics of oak, plus its pleasing variety of surface patterns, recommend it for cabinet work. Ash, birch, beech, elm, cherry, fir, maple, and spruce are also widely applied. When natural blond tones of lighter colored furniture are desired, birch, maple and spruce are particular favorites.

Woods are not always applied in the form of solid lumber. Science has made available a variety of high quality *plywoods* which are veneered with choice laminates of select wood.

Courtesy E. I. du Pont de Nemours & Co.

Courtesy E. I. du Pont de Nemours & Co

These plywoods offer the furniture maker three distinct advantages: 1) Laminated wood has greater structural stability; it is less apt to shrink, swell, warp or split. 2) Attractive graining, of matched quality, is difficult to secure with run-of-the-mill boards of solid lumber. But compatible matching of fine grain patterns may be obtained over veneered surfaces of plywood panels. 3) The cost of fine woods of select graining often inhibits their use in solid form. Plywood, surfaced with a thin veneer of select woods, is less expensive.

As already noted, contemporary materials are not limited to woods alone. Indeed, several successful contemporary furniture designers have experimented to good effect with metal, plastics, glass, and other materials.

Metal Furniture and Components

Metal furniture of fine design may lack the warmth of that made of wood. But the use of metal eliminates much bulky wooden construction. The strength of a thin metal rod can surpass that of several inches of wood. And since the metal rod may be bent to form its own joinery, much time may be saved by the manufacturer in its fabrication.

Courtesy E. I. du Pont de Nemours & Co.

Courtesy Armstrong Cork Company

Courtesy Libbey-Owens-Ford Co.

Courtesy Libbey-Owens-Ford Co.

Courtesy Hooker Furniture Corporation

As will be observed in the working chapters of this book, metal is particularly applicable for joinery of various parts of contemporary furniture. In many instances it replaces conventional wooden joints with consequent increases of strength and stability in the finished product. Metal is often used for standards and brackets of wall shelves and room dividers; for the frame structure of chests and for screw-on legs of chairs and tables. Much of the engineering of contemporary designs involves ingenious little metal fittings—steel pins, fasteners and connectors—which provide enormous strength but eliminate the bulk and complications of conventional reinforcement.

Plastic and Glass Furniture

Among other things, this has sometimes been called "The Age of Plastics." Thus, it was inevitable that some of the miraculous new synthetics would find their way into furniture fabrication. Most noteworthy are the variety of plastic chairs and tables (some of which are shown on these pages) which have appeared during recent years. These pieces are integrally molded of strong plastics to form graceful shapes. The

In his never-ending search for functional simplicity, the contemporary designer employs metal to create designs which could not be constructed, along delicate lines, of any other material. Superbly shaped chairs and tables, such as those shown on previous pages, require thin legs and bases. The strength of these designs depends on metal.

But the common-sense appeal of metal is demonstrated in its auxiliary use as a component of other materials. Metal pedestals for chairs, stools and tables, as pictured here, offer the ultimate of durability while providing a clean structure which, combined with wood and other materials, produces designs of pleasing entity. Indeed, the metal itself, when brightly plated with chromium, may add an attractive note to the decorative scheme of the contemporary interior. However, metal parts can also be painted to blend with other room colors.

Courtesy Drexel Furniture Company

molding process of plastic chairs is determined by research of comfort requirements of the human body when placed in a seated position. Thus a chair, which may have the appearance of a frail shell, is fitted exactly to body contours to provide a seat of amazing comfort. Furthermore, plastic furniture is light in weight and exceptionally durable. Usually its finish is impregnated into the plastic itself thus making it almost impervious to damage.

Going hand in hand with wood, plastics and metals, are the numerous new applications of structural glass. Until recently, glass as a component of furniture construction, was necessarily restricted to panels for doors of cabinets or, for occasional use as a protective overlay on tables and dressers where it was reinforced by solid backing.

Now, however, with the development of strong, structural glass which is virtually shatterproof, increased use is being made of this material for transparent table tops and shelving as well as doors and partitions. Because of its transparency, glass does not obstruct the space it occupies. Thus spacious tables with glass tops can be used in small room areas with only slight visual sacrifice of floor space.

Courtesy Armstrong Cork Company

Pedestal bases of chairs, tables and stools, shown above and below, are made of metal. This provides neat, light and extremely strong construction which contributes to the functional appeal of the furniture. As will be noted in Chapter 2 of this book, metal bases also simplify the job of making contemporary furniture. They can be purchased in a variety of styles and sizes and are attached with screws to quickly construct tables and other articles such as those illustrated.

Courtesy Barclay Manufacturing Co.

Courtesy Herman Miller, Inc.

Lightweight, sectional seating, has all the comfort of heavily upholstered furniture without its weight and bulk. Multiple units are mounted on platform to make sofa. But they can also be used independently for floor seating or to make the lounge chairs illustrated in Chapter 4. (See construction details in Chapter 3.) *Design by author.*

Versatile Contemporary

Designers are always striving to produce "inventive" furniture capable of serving a variety of purposes. Even Benjamin Franklin and Thomas Jefferson came up with some ingenious designs for chairs and cabinets which were original unto their concept. So, living in an era of prolific invention, many original ideas are bound to appear in the design of contemporary furniture.

One of the most noteworthy of the new attractions is the modular arrangement of sectional furniture units attached to wall standards and tension poles. As shown on pages 2 and 6, these units furnish unlimited storage space with combinations of shelving, desks, tables and cabinets of numerous purposes. As demonstrated by the various assemblies of Chapter 7, the sectional scheme serves not only to create attractive rooms but also contributes to the functional organization of these rooms.

Sectional furniture is assembled like child's blocks. Each part is fashioned as an independ-

Folding table, designed by Mogens Koch, is beautifully crafted; can be folded flat to hang on wall.

Folding chair, also designed by Koch, offers pleasing design enhanced by light weight and portability. *Courtesy Interna, Denmark*

ent piece of furniture. But it can be combined with other parts, upward and sideways, to form literally hundreds of attractive combinations. Entire walls can thus be furnished. And the units can also be latched to tension poles, reaching from floor to ceiling, to furnish the central area of the room with functional partitions and dividers.

Many ingenious advances have also been made in the manner of seating. As well as the functional chairs already noted, upholstered furniture has yielded to new techniques, making it more mobile and flexible.

The upholstered sectional seating units shown on the facing page weigh less than twenty pounds apiece. Yet they are softly upholstered with platforms of resilient webbing and full cushions of polyurethane foam. They are every bit as comfortable for relaxed seating as heavily upholstered furniture of several times their weight.

But the important appeal of this type of sectional seating is its portability and adaptability. The units can be used independently as floor seats; (a feature which is bound to delight teenagers!) or, they can be mounted on platforms of various designs to be used as lounge chairs and sofas. Their versatility is demonstrated, with working drawings in Chapters 3 and 4.

Many important innovations have also been made in the design of folding furniture. Tables and chairs such as those illustrated on the facing page, fold flat for easy storage. But they are so neatly designed that they do not take on the appearance of "novelty" furniture when used in conventional room settings.

Other designs such as the convertible table, pictured at the right, are made to serve multiple purposes. Primarily this functions as a spacious coffee table. But it is hinged across the middle to fold up to seating height and may thus be used for dining and working as well as a handy card and game table.

The obvious advantage of such designs is that a single article of furniture serves many requirements and thus conserves room space which would otherwise be absorbed by additional pieces of single purpose.

"Tumble-Table" spreads out before sofa as a spacious coffee table. But by folding it into upright position, gravity holds two ends firmly together to form utility table for dining or working. (See construction details in Chapter 3) *Design by author.*

Arrival of a Mature Contemporary Style

The many illustrations of individual contemporary designs and blending of these designs into the attractive interiors shown in this book indicate that contemporary furniture has already progressed beyond the experimental stage and now identifies itself as a dignified and mature style of furniture. Expanding beyond its Scandinavian origins, it is now manufactured throughout the world.

There's no question about the beauty and fitness of this furniture. Its modest, sculptured lines compliment the rooms in which it is used. And its functional efficiency contributes to the ease and comfort of modern living.

Looking back over the principal periods and styles of furniture, and probing the reasons why they have remained in prominence, it is possible to equate their sanity of approach with what is happening to furniture today. For this is sound stuff. And the contemporary designer approaches his problems with no less restraint than that exercised by the distinguished designers of centuries past.

Thus the contemporary style is here to stay —and, from all indications, in the future it will take its place among other renowned furniture styles of traditional distinction.

Courtesy Royal System

2

BASIC CONTEMPORARY PROJECTS

BASIC CONTEMPORARY
PROJECTS

Many people with do-it-yourself inclinations find themselves inhibited about getting into furniture building because they regard this as an advanced craft requiring the special skills and training of a cabinetmaker. Indeed, to an extent they are right. For certainly some of the projects presented in this book do require a considerable degree of woodworking ability. And the tools and equipment needed for their construction would only be contained in the home workshop of the advanced woodworking hobbyist.

But this does not mean that the average householder cannot successfully make many of the projects shown here. This is particularly true of the basic contemporary projects presented in this chapter.

In many instances these projects require little more in the way of skill than the ability to assemble stock materials. For the most part they do not demand an outlay for elaborate tools and equipment. In fact, the normal assortment of household tools should suffice for this construction.

All of these projects are designed to be *functional*. They will serve you and your family and make welcome additions to the furnishing of your home. Furthermore, you can save yourself much money by making them. For the materials involved cost only the smallest fraction of the value of the finished pieces.

Because of its simplicity of design and construction, basic contemporary furniture is, of itself, easy to make. It does not require elaborate shaping or turning of parts. Most of it is built board on board—with the graining characteristics of the wood providing its own natural enrichment. Simplicity keynotes its design. And its inherent simplicity of design offers the advantage of ease of construction for those who would make it themselves.

Availability of Standard Parts

As will be noted in the projects which follow, most of this furniture is assembled of standard parts which may be purchased economically at your lumber and hardware dealers. Boards, cut to required lengths (which your lumber dealer will do for you) are attached to metal brackets to make convenient shelves. Plywood panels, simply sawed to size, are assembled with attachable legs to make attractive and useful tables. Standard, flush panel doors, which can be bought for a few dollars apiece, are assembled with standard legs and metal pedestals to form tables, desks, beds and seating platforms. Thus, at minimum price of stock parts, you can assemble attractive furniture which might otherwise cost hundreds of dollars.

And with this furniture the maker need not feel that he or she is settling for something "improvised" and second-best. Each piece presented here contributes to the good taste and functional organization of the home in which it is used.

So why not try your hand at making some of the pieces shown here? In particular, "young marrieds" who have a budget to maintain, will find considerable savings in their do-it-yourself enterprise. At your local lumber and hardware dealer you will find all the materials and standard accessories needed to make these projects.

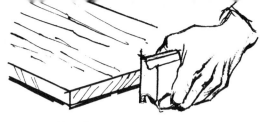
Sanding End Grain

TO BUILD
WITH BOARDS

Starting with the simplest materials, it is easy to make a number of attractive and practical household projects. For instance, most homes lack adequate shelving. Perhaps a utility shelf is needed in the kitchen or bathroom. Certainly, there's nothing easier than to buy a board of required width and length, attach it to metal brackets, and mount it on the wall. And this offers a clue to the ease of making most projects in this chapter.

You may also need a folding breakfast counter which tucks down against the wall and out of the way when not in use. Make it yourself with a board and folding brackets. That overflow of books in your living room may need additional shelves and containers. So follow the plans, of following pages, and assemble them to suit your needs.

Thus with boards alone, which you can saw off yourself—or, get sawed to size by your lumber dealer—you can make a variety of tables, counters, stools, telephone nooks, book bins and shelves. And all you will need to complete the job are a few incidentals of hardware.

But even boards require a bit of elementary crafting if they are to look right. So get some sandpaper and smooth them thoroughly as shown in the accompanying sketches.

If your home is furnished with the finer contemporary woods, such as teak and walnut, you may want to spend the extra to buy boards of such species. Or, you may prefer to buy plywood, veneered with fine woods. But if your projects are to be painted you need not be concerned with the color and surface characteristics of the boards you use. However, you should specify a good grade of lumber which will not warp or split. For finishing your board projects, follow the instructions of Chapter 9.

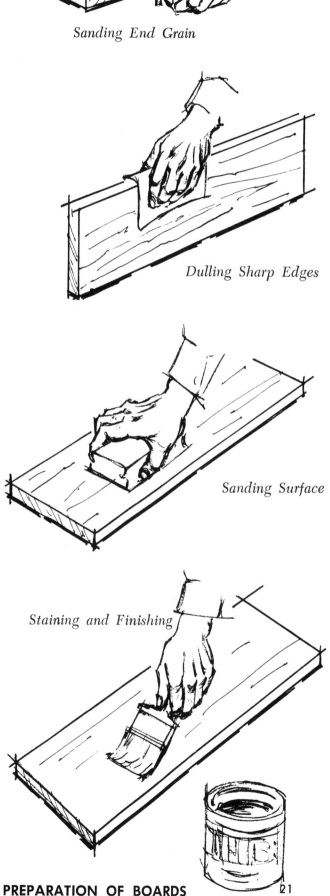
Dulling Sharp Edges

Sanding Surface

Staining and Finishing

PREPARATION OF BOARDS

21

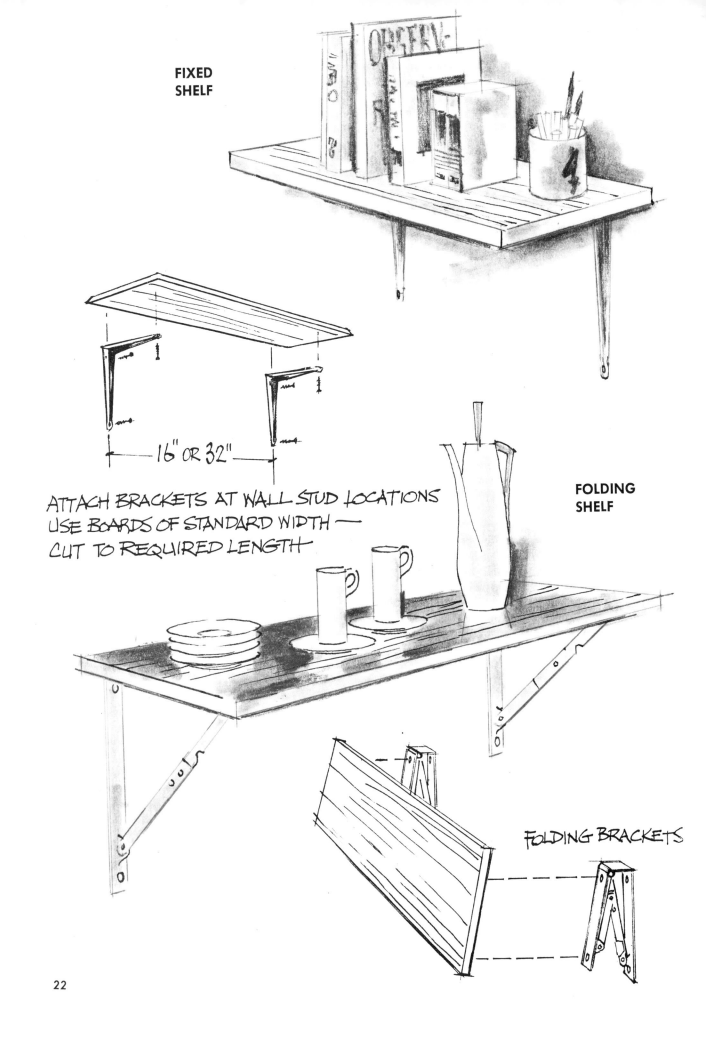

FIXED SHELF

16" OR 32"

ATTACH BRACKETS AT WALL STUD LOCATIONS
USE BOARDS OF STANDARD WIDTH —
CUT TO REQUIRED LENGTH

FOLDING SHELF

FOLDING BRACKETS

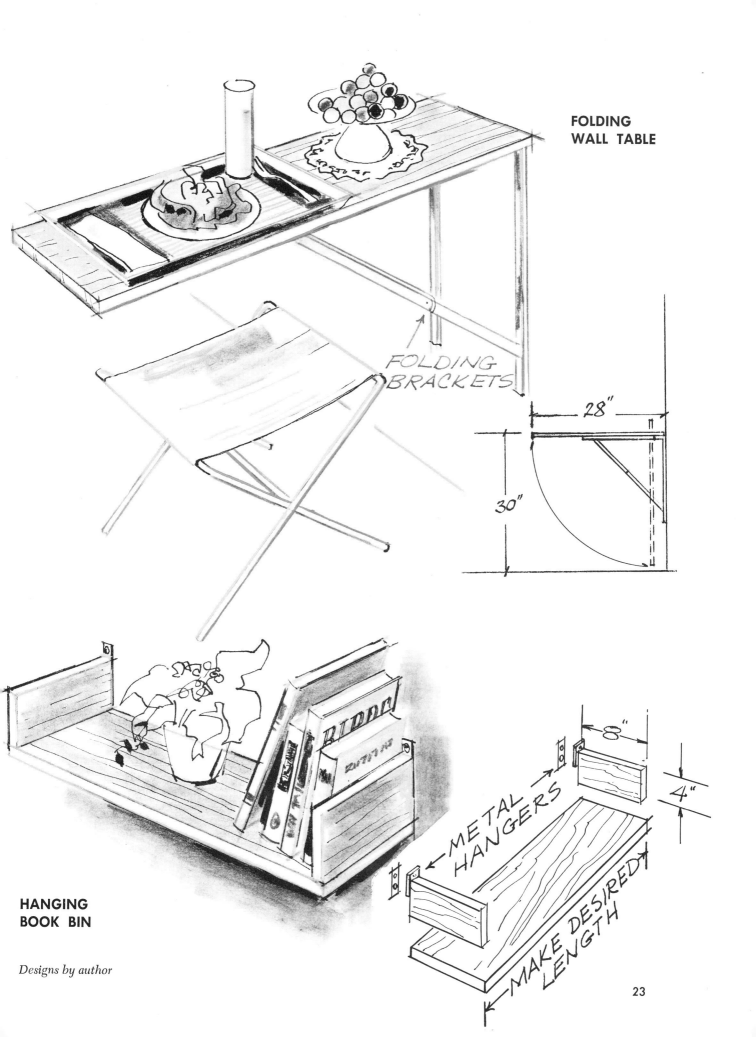

**FOLDING
WALL TABLE**

FOLDING
BRACKETS

28"

30"

**HANGING
BOOK BIN**

METAL
HANGERS

8"

4"

MAKE DESIRED
LENGTH

Designs by author

23

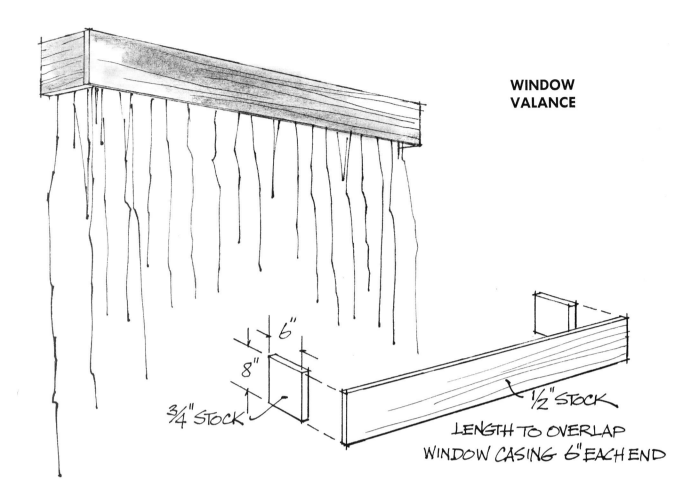

WINDOW VALANCE

6"

8"

3/4" STOCK

1/2" STOCK

LENGTH TO OVERLAP
WINDOW CASING 6" EACH END

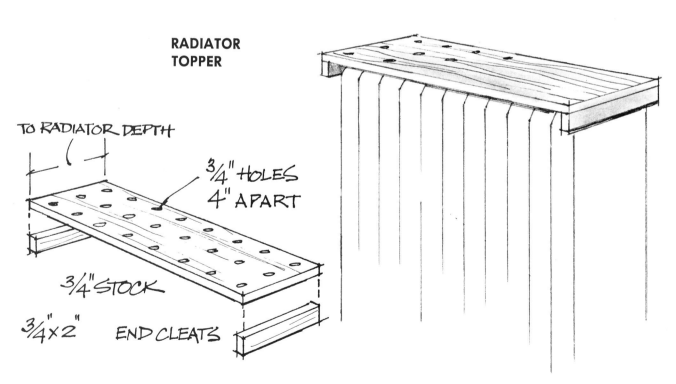

RADIATOR TOPPER

TO RADIATOR DEPTH

3/4" HOLES
4" APART

3/4" STOCK

3/4" x 2" END CLEATS

PIE TABLES

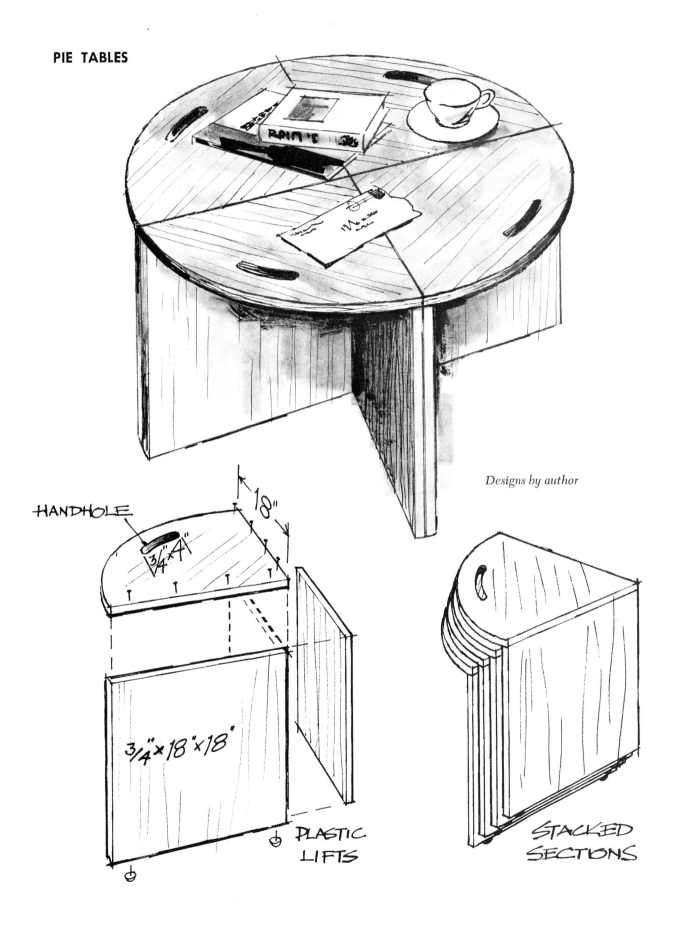

Designs by author

HANDHOLE

3/4" × 4"

18"

3/4" × 18" × 18"

PLASTIC
LIFTS

STACKED
SECTIONS

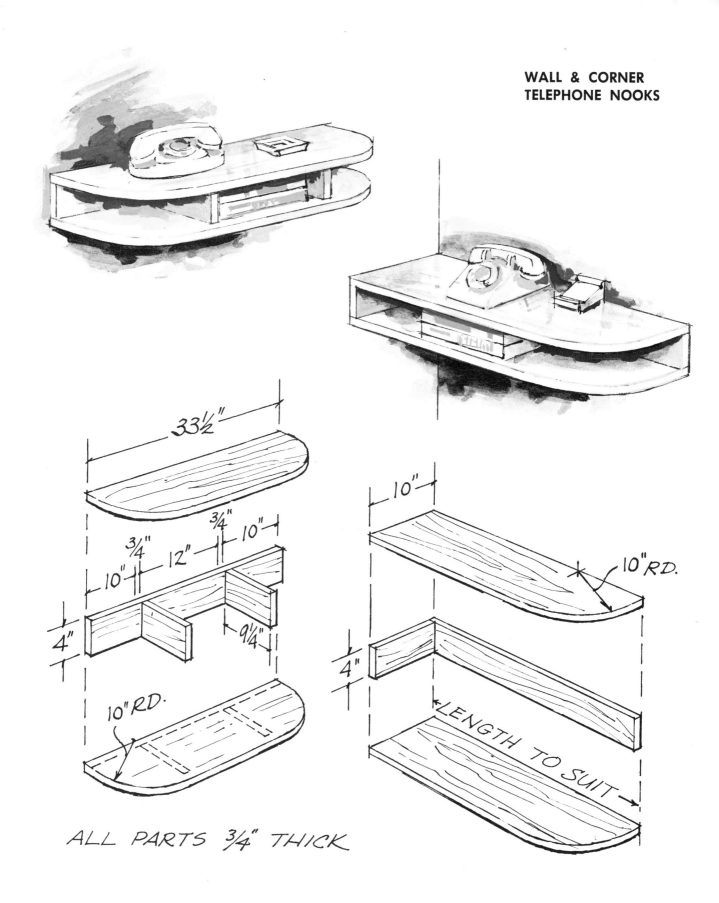

33½"

¾"

10" 12" ¾" 10"

4" 9¼"

10"RD.

10"

10"RD.

4"

LENGTH TO SUIT

ALL PARTS ¾" THICK

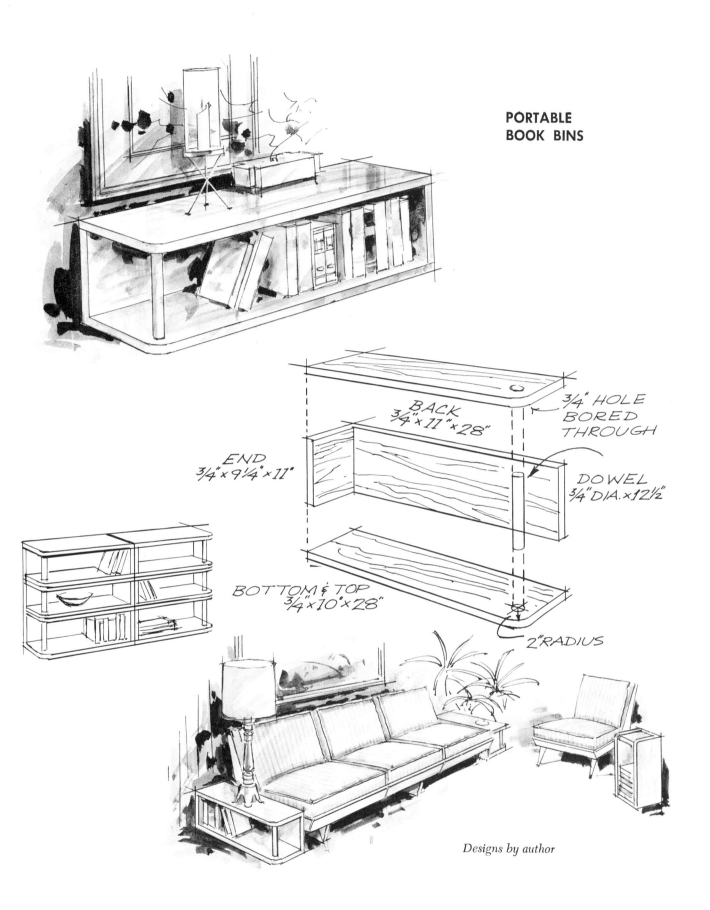

**PORTABLE
BOOK BINS**

BACK
3/4" x 11" x 28"

3/4" HOLE
BORED
THROUGH

END
3/4" x 9 1/4" x 11"

DOWEL
3/4" DIA. x 12 1/2"

BOTTOM & TOP
3/4" x 10" x 28"

2" RADIUS

Designs by author

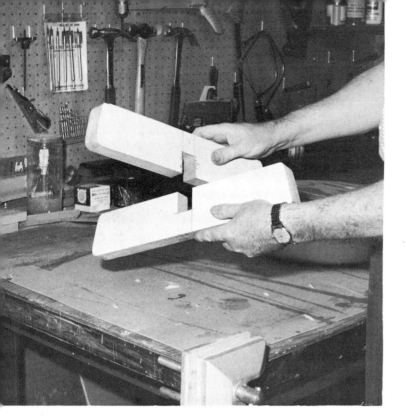

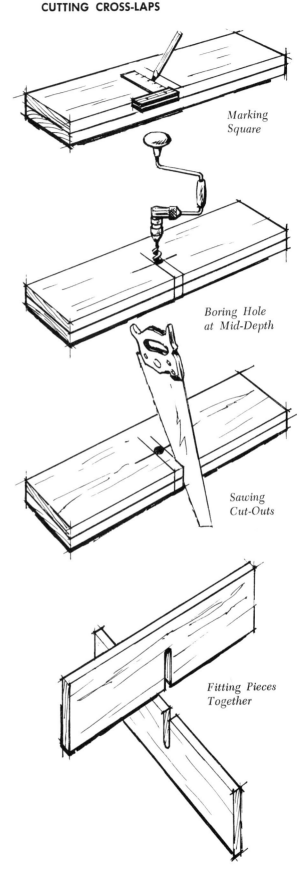

Marking Square

Boring Hole at Mid-Depth

Sawing Cut-Outs

Fitting Pieces Together

CROSS-LAP CONSTRUCTION

Perhaps the uninitiated would prefer to call this "egg crate" construction. For the cross-lap joint fits exactly the same as the overlapping cardboard separators used in old-fashioned egg crates.

This joint is commonly used in contemporary construction. And on the basis of simply fitting together a couple of overlapping boards, a variety of attractive projects can be made.

The only tools you need to cut a cross-lap are the saw and brace and bit. You can even do without the brace and bit if you saw evenly to remove the cut-out portion. Follow the sketches at the right to cut your cross-laps.

About the only word of warning needed by the amateur craftsman is to saw precisely *to the line*. If the sawing spreads beyond the thickness of the joining board, a wobbly and insecure joint will result. (If you have had no experience at this, try your hand with a couple of pieces of scrapwood.)

Once you have mastered the art of cross-lapping, you can go on to make the many attractive projects which follow.

CROSS-LAP
FOOTSTOOLS

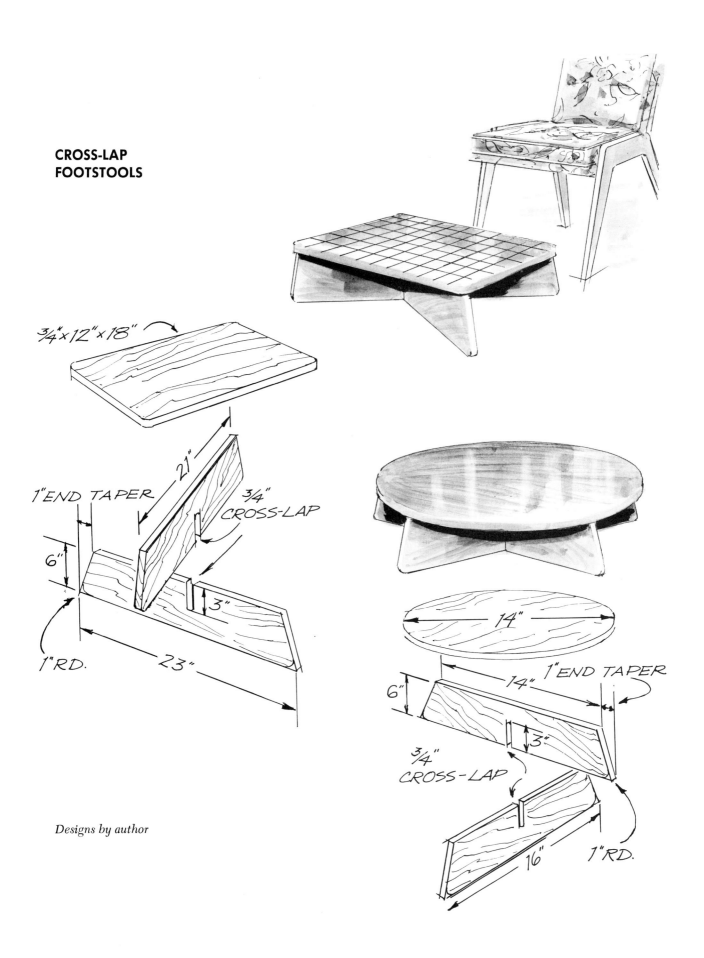

3/4" x 12" x 18"

1" END TAPER

3/4" CROSS-LAP

6"

3"

1" RD.

23"

21"

Designs by author

14"

1" END TAPER

14"

6"

3"

3/4" CROSS-LAP

16"

1" RD.

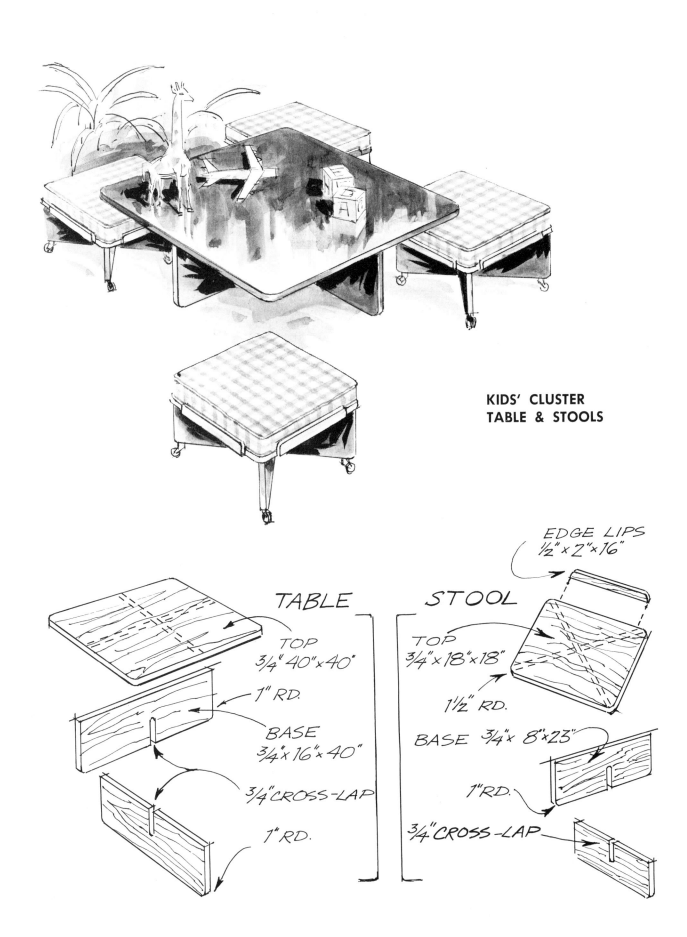

**KIDS' CLUSTER
TABLE & STOOLS**

TABLE

TOP
3/4" 40"x40"

1" RD.

BASE
3/4" x 16" x 40"

3/4" CROSS-LAP

1" RD.

STOOL

EDGE LIPS
1/2" x 2" x 16"

TOP
3/4" x 18" x 18"

1 1/2" RD.

BASE 3/4" x 8" x 23"

1" RD.

3/4" CROSS-LAP

**CROSS-LAP
COMPANIONS**

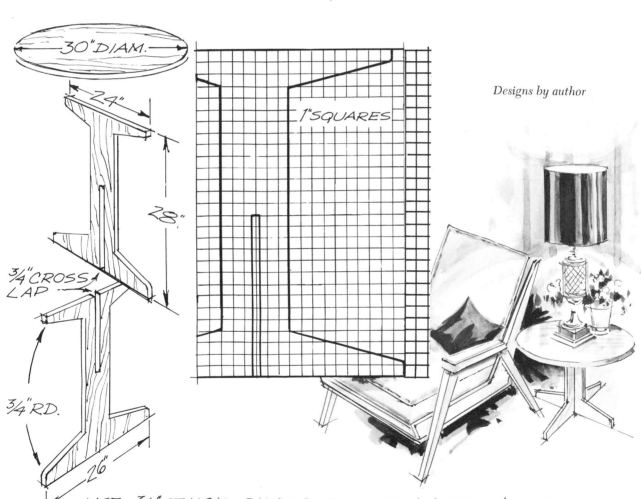

30" DIAM.

24"

1" SQUARES

28"

3/4" CROSS
LAP

3/4" RD.

26"

Designs by author

USE 3/4" THICK PLYWOOD FOR LARGE & SMALL
DESIGNS — REDUCE DIMENSIONS 1/2 FOR
STOOLS & SMALL TABLE.

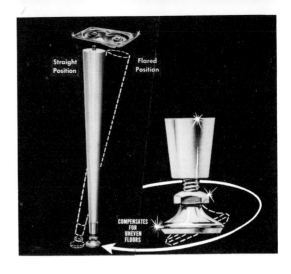

TO ASSEMBLE
WITH ATTACHABLE LEGS

As illustrated on this page, attachable legs can be obtained in a variety of types and sizes. They are made of both metal and wood. Of the wooden variety, they come finished or unfinished and are made of many woods, including teak and walnut, to match your projects. Metal legs are usually painted black but can be repainted to any desired color. Some are finished in brass and chromium.

To attach these legs you simply drive a few screws through the top plates. Some, like the Gerber legs, shown at the right, come with detachable plates threaded for assembly of the legs either in perpendicular or slanted positions. The legs are then screwed to the plates with a threaded spindle. They have adjustable nylon, leveling disks threaded to the bottom tips. These are adjusted to eliminate wobbling on uneven floors.

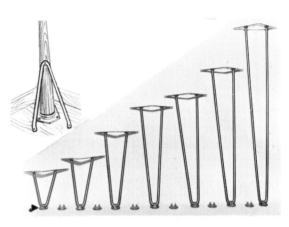

Courtesy Gerber Wrought Iron Products, Inc.

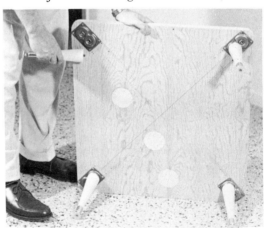

Courtesy The Door Store, Washington, D.C.

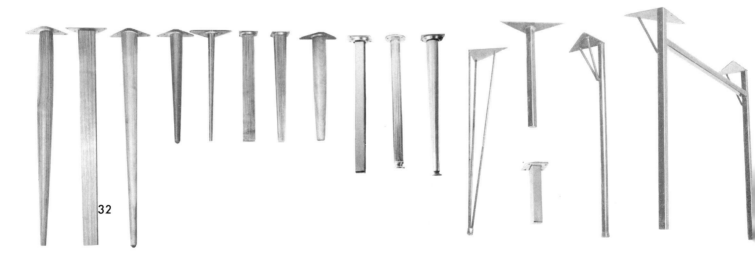

32

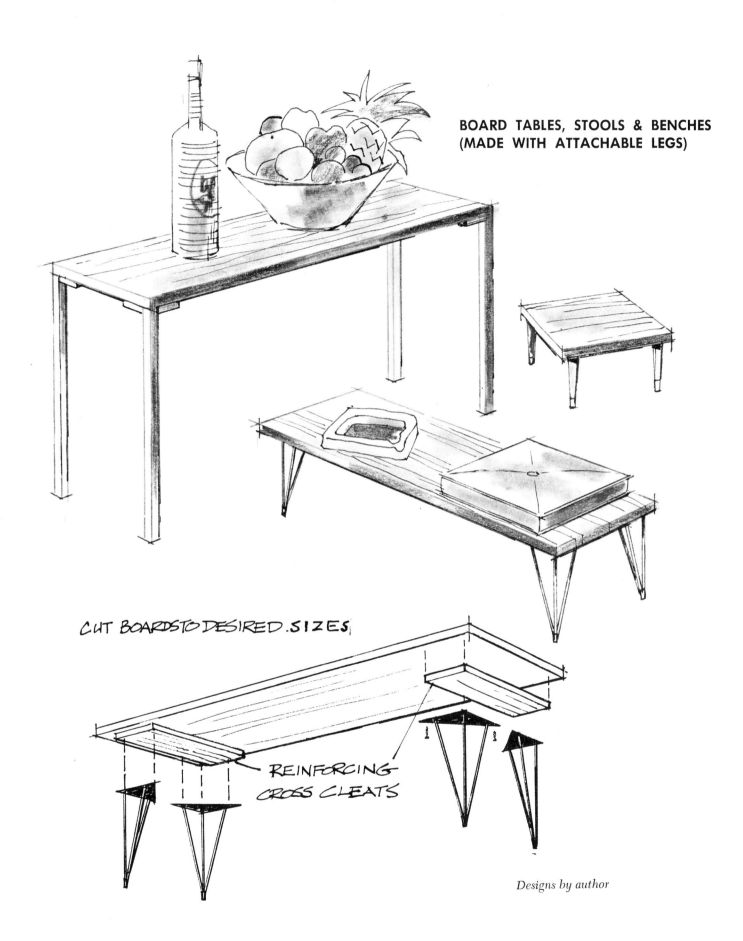

**BOARD TABLES, STOOLS & BENCHES
(MADE WITH ATTACHABLE LEGS)**

CUT BOARDS TO DESIRED SIZES

REINFORCING CROSS CLEATS

Designs by author

33

**SOFA PLATFORM &
PEG-LEG TABLES**

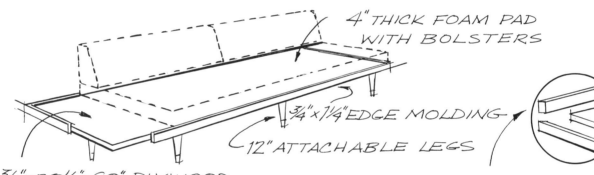

4" THICK FOAM PAD
WITH BOLSTERS

3/4" x 1 1/4" EDGE MOLDING

12" ATTACHABLE LEGS

3/4" x 28 1/2" x 90" PLYWOOD

MITER MOLDING
GLUE & NAIL TO
TOP EDGES

3/4" x 24" x 60"
PLYWOOD TOP

3/4" x 18" x 18" TOP

1/2" x 1 1/2" EDGE MOLDING

3/8" x 1 1/2"
MOLDING

12" ATTACHABLE LEGS

10" ATTACHABLE IRON LEGS

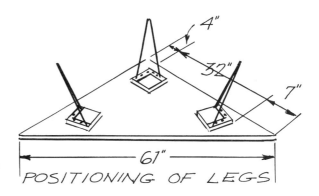

4"

32"

7"

|← 61" →|

POSITIONING OF LEGS

4 TOPS & LEG PADS CUT
FROM STANDARD 4'x8' SHEET
OF EXTERIOR-GRADE PLYWOOD

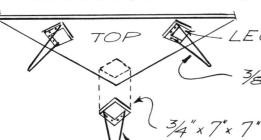

TOP — LEG PAD

3/8" WROUGHT IRON LEGS

3/4" x 7" x 7" LEG PADS

16" LEGS FOR LOW TABLES

28" LEGS FOR PICNIC TABLES

QUAD TABLES

Courtesy Gerber Wrought Iron Products, Inc.

TO ASSEMBLE WITH PEDESTAL BASES

If you want to make a table, chair or stool in a hurry, there's nothing will hasten the job more effectively than the pedestal bases pictured on these pages. These bases are made of metal and can be bolted together in a jiffy.

As illustrated above, the top plate is pre-drilled to be screwed to an attaching surface. Thus, to make tables like those shown here, it is only necessary to fashion a top of plywood to desired dimensions and attach it to the pedestal base with six screws. Stools and chairs are almost as easily assembled.

Pedestal bases may be purchased in two sizes: 14″ tall for low tables, stools and chairs and 28″ tall for full size tables. They are finished either in brass or enamel and can be refinished to match any desired color scheme.

With these pedestals it is possible for even the complete beginner to assemble attractive furniture at nominal cost. They can be purchased at most hardware stores or from do-it-yourself dealers.

Chair-side tables are quickly assembled with 14″ Gerber pedestal bases. The one above was made with a 24″ disk of ¾″ plywood. Edges were rounded and all parts vinyl finished. The square-topped design, below, was made with a 20″ square of prefinished walnut wall paneling, laminated over a panel of ordinary ½″ plywood. Top edges are finished to match the base.

Designs by author

The illustration at the right demonstrates what can be done with pedestal bases to produce furniture which would cost several times as much as the components of its construction. The table top is made of a 36″ disk of ¾″ plywood. (For rich results use plywood veneered with walnut or teak and cover the edges with matching Welwood veneer tape.) The chairs are constructed to the dimensions of plan shown below.

However, if you feel the making of these chairs goes a bit beyond your ability as a craftsman, why not substitute round-top stools? They can be made with ¾″ plywood disks and covered with standard cushions like those shown on page 45. In this way you can assemble an attractive and expensive looking dining group for the cost of the pedestals and plywood. The top circles are cut with a coping saw or jig saw. But if you don't own such tools and can't borrow them, your lumber dealer will probably be glad to bandsaw them for you. Even so, you will be way ahead on costs—and your friends will call you clever!

Designs by author

PEDESTAL TABLE & CHAIRS

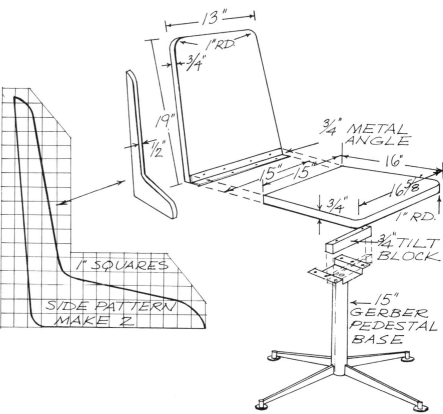

37

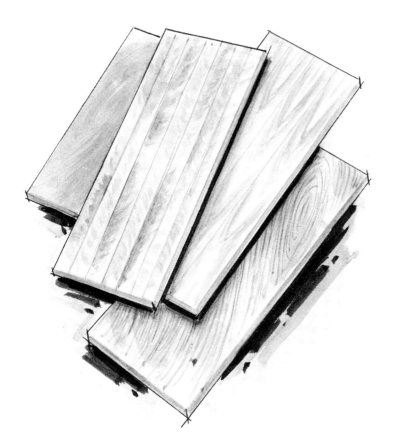

TO DO WITH DOORS

Flush panel doors—the plain kind that you can buy unfinished, at any lumber yard or from building supply dealers—are used to make a multitude of attractive and useful articles of furniture. They are most commonly made in lengths of 80″ and in widths, graduating by 2″, from 18″ to 36″. Surfaces are laminated of thin plywood with Philippine mahogany, birch, and maple most commonly used. Some are surfaced with Masonite for painting, and they can also be purchased in richer woods.

Most flush doors are "stuffed" with wood staves bonded diagonally within the panel surfaces. Since these staves are spaced to form a hollow core, fastenings cannot be made within the hollow areas. Thus when legs are attached, cleats are glued to span the under surface and fastened, with screws, along the solid edges.

Edges are usually made of a soft wood and should be covered with thin molding strips matching the surface or with edge veneer tape of similar wood. The accompanying step-by-step photo sequence shows how flush doors are cut down to required lengths.

How to Reduce Lengths of Flush Doors

1 Door is sawed to required length. Use fine-tooth crosscut saw.

2 Diagonal staves of hollow core appear in sawed-off section.

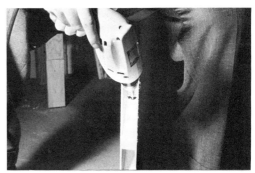

3 Drill is used to sever staves within margin of panel edges.

4 Stave ends are removed with chisel. Tap gently to avoid surface splitting.

5 Glue is applied to inner surfaces of panels. Cover entire exposed area.

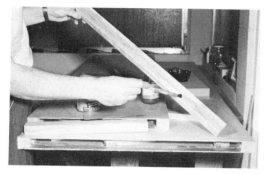

6 Edge stave is glued to insert between panels. Make new stave 1¼″ thick on surface.

7 Glued stave is tapped into place. Piece must be exact thickness of inner staves.

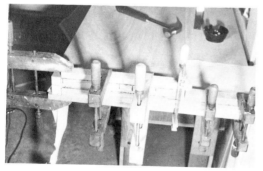

8 Reinforced end is clamped until glue dries and then planed flush.

DOOR TABLE

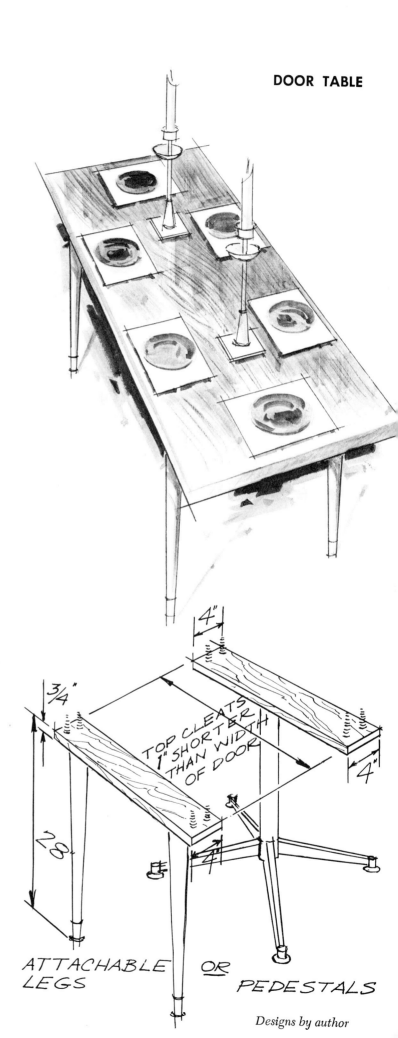

TOP CLEATS 1″ SHORTER THAN WIDTH OF DOOR

4″

3/4″

28″

4″

4″

ATTACHABLE LEGS   OR   PEDESTALS

Designs by author

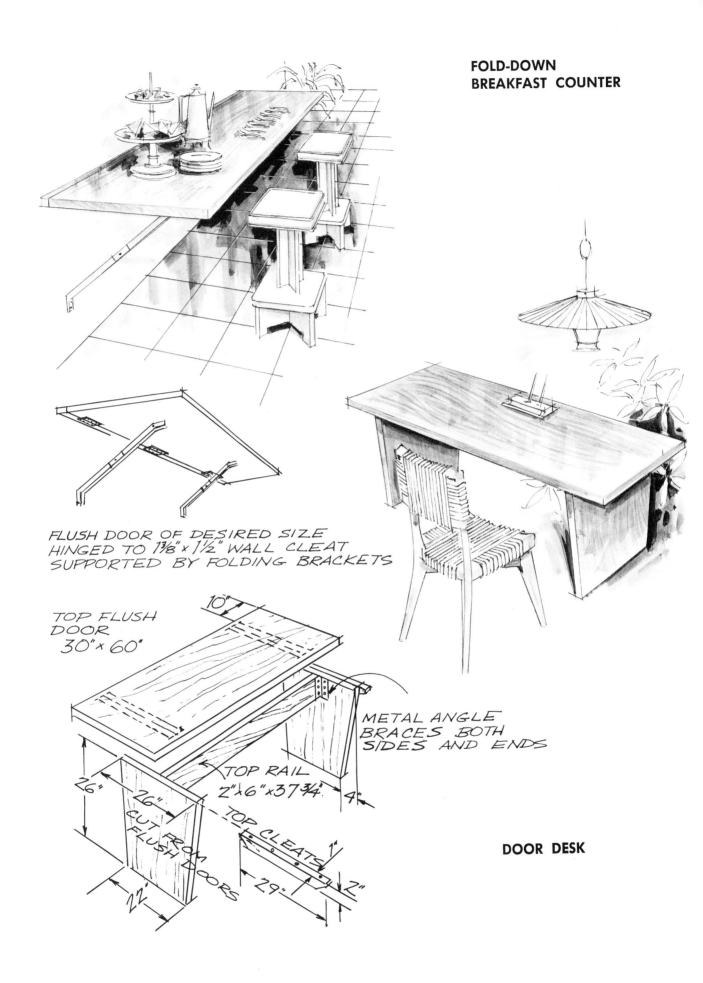

FLUSH DOOR OF DESIRED SIZE
HINGED TO 1⅜" x 1½" WALL CLEAT
SUPPORTED BY FOLDING BRACKETS

TOP FLUSH
DOOR
30" x 60"

10"

METAL ANGLE
BRACES BOTH
SIDES AND ENDS

TOP RAIL
2" x 6" x 37¾"

4"

26"

26"
CUT FROM
FLUSH DOORS

TOP CLEATS

1"

2"

22"

29"

DOOR DESK

FOLDING DOOR SCREEN

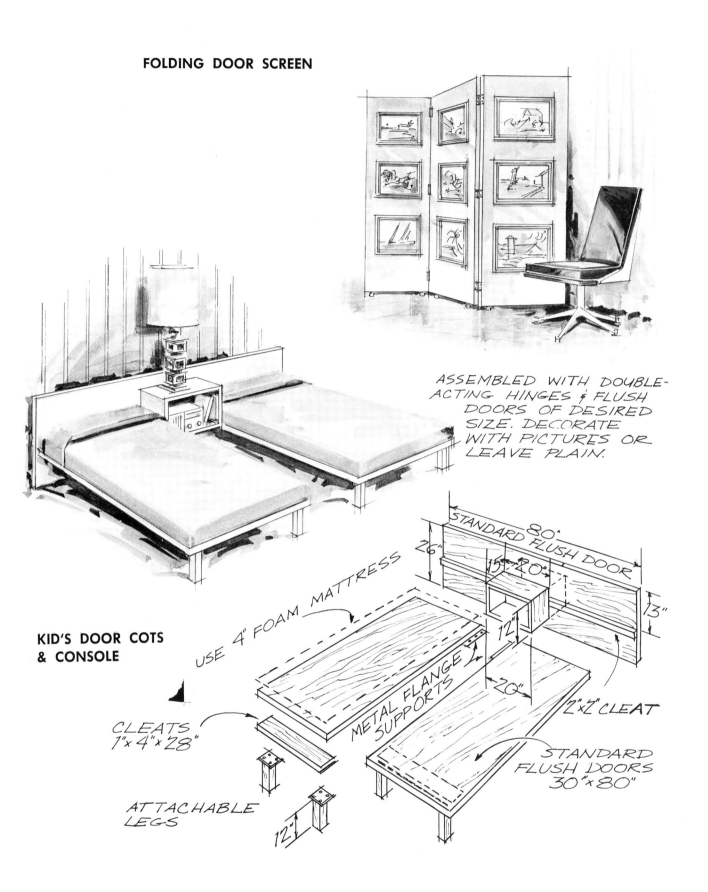

ASSEMBLED WITH DOUBLE-ACTING HINGES & FLUSH DOORS OF DESIRED SIZE. DECORATE WITH PICTURES OR LEAVE PLAIN.

KID'S DOOR COTS & CONSOLE

USE 4" FOAM MATTRESS

METAL FLANGE SUPPORTS

80"

STANDARD FLUSH DOOR

26"

15" 20"

12"

3"

20"

2"x2" CLEAT

STANDARD FLUSH DOORS 30"x80"

CLEATS 1"x 4"x 28"

ATTACHABLE LEGS

12"

Designs by author

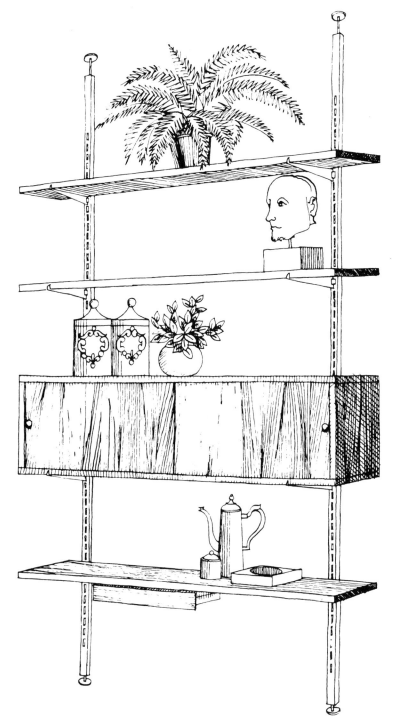

TO ASSEMBLE WITH STANDARDS, SHELVES AND TENSION POLES

An abundance of bright, new hardware has paved the way for ambitious do-it-yourselfers to create many attractive interior effects. We have already observed how attachable legs and metal pedestals assist the amateur to make furniture. But there are other items available at your hardware or specialty shop which offer additional help.

Take the wall shelving and shelved room dividers shown on these pages: These useful and highly decorative effects can be had by simply mounting shelves or cases on metal wall standards or spring-loaded tension poles which reach from floor to ceiling.

The hardware which produces these effects comes in a variety of makes, styles and sizes. The wall standards are attached over wall studding as demonstrated in Chapter 7. They are slotted to receive keyed metal brackets on which the shelf boards are mounted.

Tension poles which fit snugly between floor and ceiling do not require special installation. Of course, they must be kept in alignment and adjusted to fit perpendicular to the floor.

This hardware can be bought separately—or, you can buy complete kits containing hardware and wooden components.

Shelves and cases are mounted on metal brackets and supported by spring-loaded tension poles to make this attractive room divider. *Courtesy The Door Store, Washington, D.C.*

Supporting brackets which anchor in slots of wall standards can be obtained for horizontal mounting or with adjustable pivot for slanted shelving. *Courtesy The Door Store, Washington, D.C.*

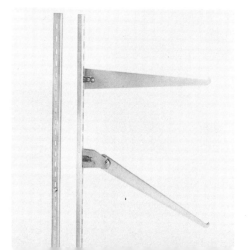

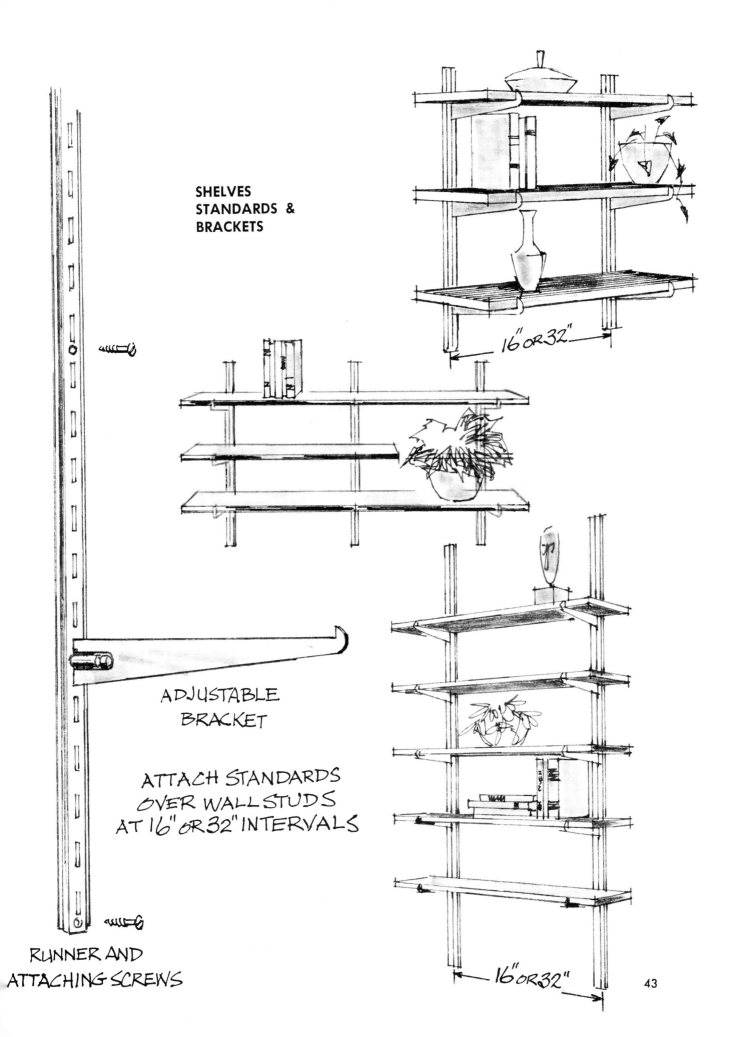

**SHELVES
STANDARDS &
BRACKETS**

16" OR 32"

ADJUSTABLE
BRACKET

ATTACH STANDARDS
OVER WALL STUDS
AT 16" OR 32" INTERVALS

16" OR 32"

RUNNER AND
ATTACHING SCREWS

43

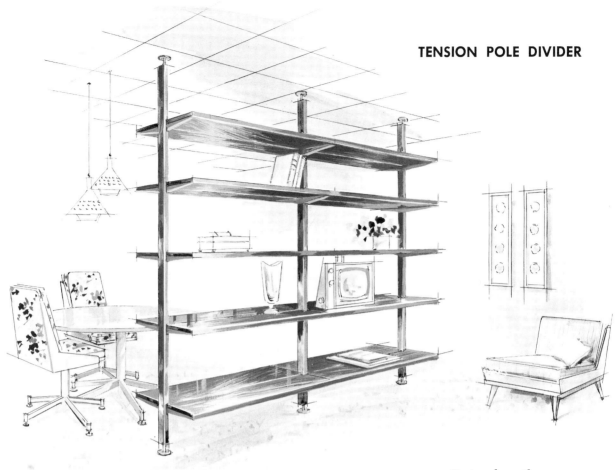

Designs by author

MAKE YOUR OWN TENSION POLES, BRACKETS AND SHELVES

If you are one of those skilled homecrafters who prefers to do it entirely yourself without recourse to specialized hardware, you can make your own tension poles and build the room dividers and other sectional shelving effects shown in this book. In fact, by so doing, you will save a considerable amount of money.

The shelved divider illustrated above is made of standard lumber—stock "two-by-threes" for the tension poles and ¾″ boards for the shelves and brackets. The construction involved is relatively simple.

Following the working drawing on the facing page, select straight two-by-threes and saw them to required lengths. Bore one end with a 1³⁄₁₆″ bit to receive free-fitting ¾″ spring dowels. (Dowel at the floor end is stationary and should be bored for exact fit.) Then bore ¼″ holes at 3″ intervals, along the center to receive wing bolts which hold adjustable shelf brackets.

The brackets are made with lapped ends to measurements shown on plan. It will be noted single (one-arm) brackets are specified for mounting of one-sided wall shelving. Shelves are notched to fit corners of tension poles to measurements indicated. Double shelving, for divider shown above, requires shallower notching for reciprocal fitting as shown in variation of plan.

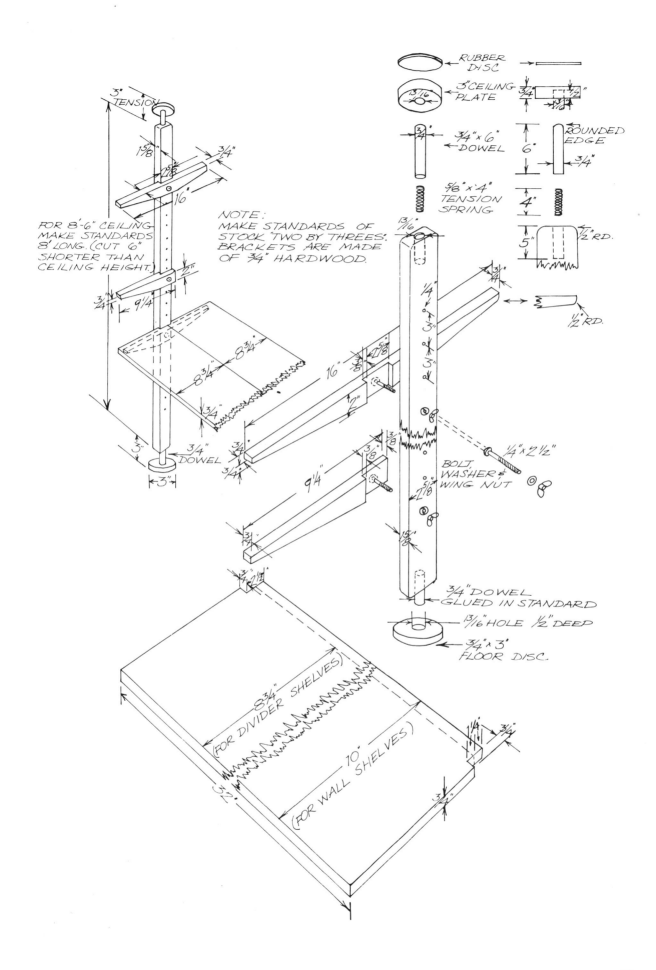

RUBBER DISC

3" CEILING PLATE

3/4"

1/2"

3/4" x 6" DOWEL

ROUNDED EDGE

3/4"

6"

5/8" x 4" TENSION SPRING

4"

5"

1/2" RD.

1/2" RD.

3" TENSION

1 5/8"

2 5/8"

3/4"

16"

FOR 8'-6" CEILING MAKE STANDARDS 8' LONG. (CUT 6" SHORTER THAN CEILING HEIGHT.)

NOTE: MAKE STANDARDS OF STOCK "TWO BY THREES". BRACKETS ARE MADE OF 3/4" HARDWOOD.

13/16"

1/4"

3"

3"

3/4"

2"

9 1/4"

3/4"

3/4"

8 3/4"

8 3/4"

8 3/4"

3/4"

16"

5/8"

5/8"

1/4" x 2 1/2" BOLT, WASHER & WING NUT

3"

3/4" DOWEL

3/4"

3/4"

3/8"

3/8"

9 1/4"

3/8"

3/4"

2 1/8"

5"

1 5/8"

3"

2 1/8"

3/4" DOWEL GLUED IN STANDARD

13/16" HOLE 1/2" DEEP

3/4" x 3" FLOOR DISC.

8 3/4" (FOR DIVIDER SHELVES)

10" (FOR WALL SHELVES)

32"

10"

1/4"

3/4"

3/4"

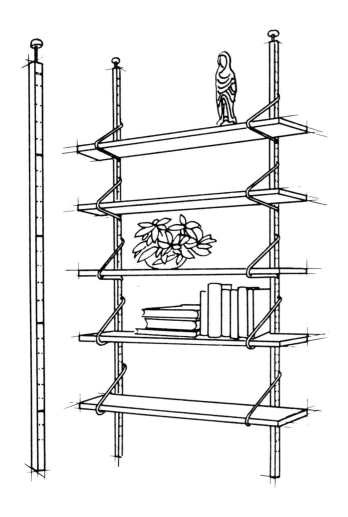

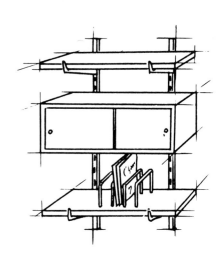

VARIATIONS WITH METAL FITTINGS

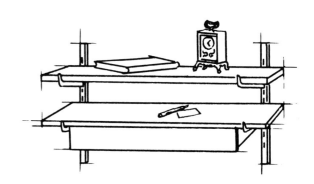

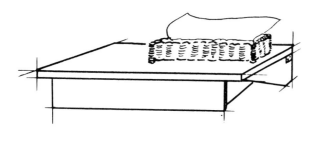

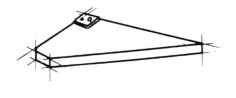

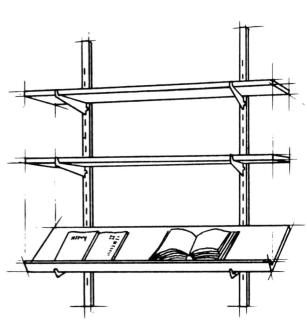

Courtesy The Door Store, Washington, D.C.

3

HOW TO BUILD CONTEMPORARY FURNITURE— STEP-BY-STEP

Basic hand tools courtesy Millers Falls Co.

HOW TO MAKE
A BUFFET STOOL
WITH HAND TOOLS

Original design by author

You really don't need a huge inventory of tools to make many of the projects shown in this book. In fact, if you own only the basic assortment illustrated above, you can get along quite nicely. To demonstrate this, the buffet stool was built entirely with these tools and photographed in step-by-step construction sequence along the way. This is a practical stool for kitchen or workroom. Its construction follows the simple cross-lap principle described in the previous chapter. Plywood is used for all surface parts. If you would rather have round stools, substitute 18½″ disks for the square top and base plate. As well as guiding the construction of the stool, the following sequence of photographs should also serve as a ready source reference in hand tool operations.

Cross-lap buffet stools provide a sturdy perch beside a breakfast counter or can be used at a work table. Following same construction, center parts can be cut 18" long to make low stools for use beside conventional tables. Top cushions, of foam, bring extra comfort.

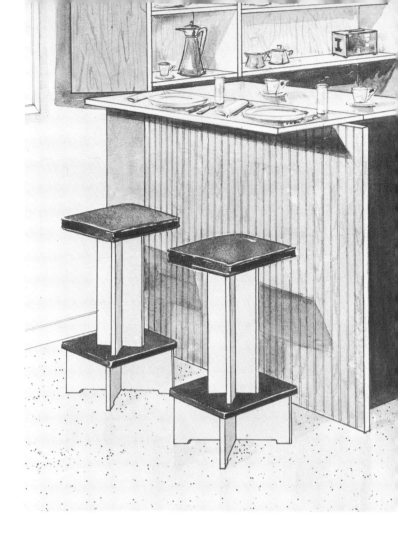

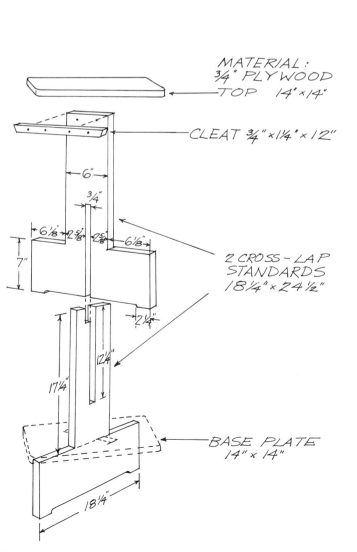

MATERIAL:
3/4" PLYWOOD
TOP 14" x 14"

CLEAT 3/4" x 1 1/4" x 12"

6"

3/4"

6 1/8" — 2 5/8" — 2 5/8" — 6 1/8"

7"

2 CROSS-LAP STANDARDS
18 1/4" x 24 1/2"

2 1/4"

12 1/4"

17 1/4"

BASE PLATE
14" x 14"

18 1/4"

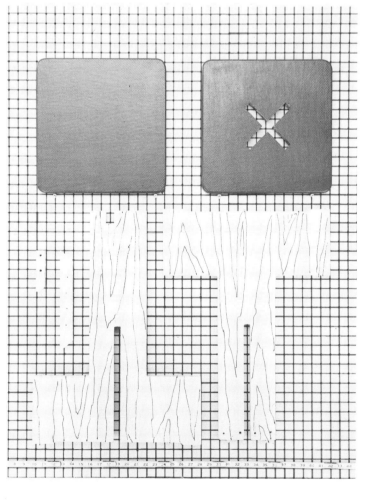

1 Mark parts on plywood from cardboard pattern.

2 Square marking for absolute accuracy.

3 Crosscut just outside lines of marking.

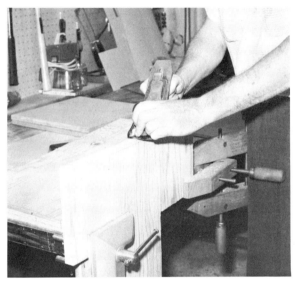

4 Plane two standards to lines of marking.

5 Smooth with sandpaper; dull all sharp edges.

6 Bore ¾" hole at terminal of center cross-lap marking.

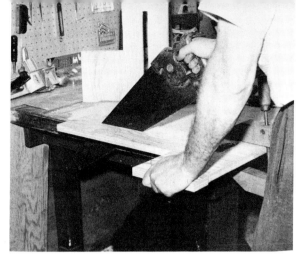

7 Saw cross-lap cutouts from opposite ends of standards.

8 Trim inside of cutouts with sharp chisel.

9 Coping saw trims ¼" hollow at base of standards.

10 Cross-lap standards are fitted together.

11 Marking for "X" cutout of base plate is made from standards.

12 Boring of "X" cutout is performed with ¾" bit.

13 Keyhole or compass saw removes cutout area.

14 File is used to trim "X" cutout.

15 Coping saw notches end of one standard to receive top cleat.

16 Base plate is fitted over assembled standards.

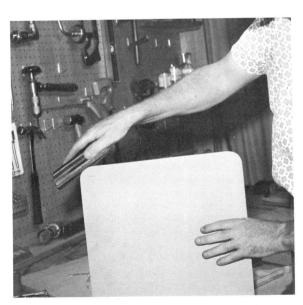

17 Sanding block is used to smooth rounded corners.

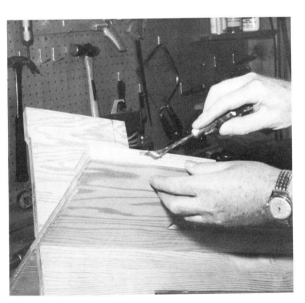

18 Gaps in plywood edges are filled with plastic wood.

19 Top cleat is fastened with screws and glue.

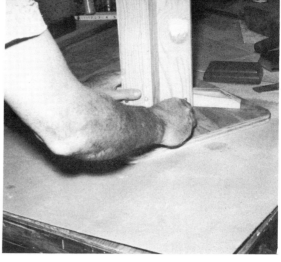

20 Standards are fastened to top cleat with screws and glue.

21 Assembled stool is thoroughly sanded; all edges dulled and rounded.

22 Pad of 2″ foam can be tacked to top with tabbed cover.

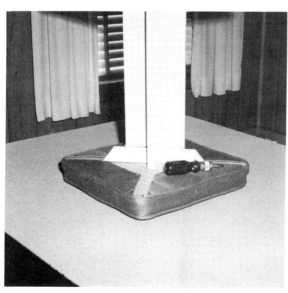

23 Upholstered top is secured to base. (See upholstering detail, Chapter 8.)

24 Finished buffet stool is painted in contrasting colors.

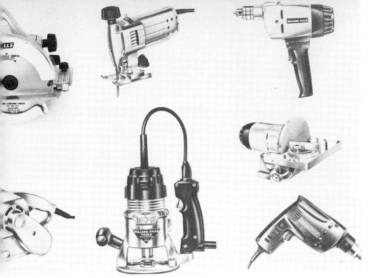

Portable power tools, courtesy Millers Falls Co.

HOW TO MAKE
SECTIONAL SEATING UNITS
WITH PORTABLE POWER TOOLS

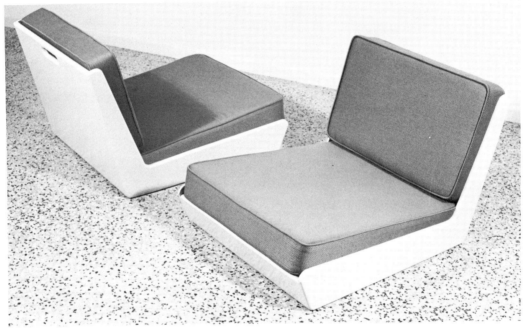

Original design by author

Your investment in portable power tools, such as those illustrated above, will pay off in prompt production of attractive furniture. For with power you can perform, *in minutes* what may require hours to do by hand. Furthermore, you generally get greater accuracy with power tools. In construction of the Sectional Seating Units shown in step-by step photo sequences of following pages, all of these power tools play a part. Considering the cost of upholstered furniture, in relation to the multiple applications of such seating units, their production will soon repay the price of the tools. The operations performed in the following pictures also apply to construction of other furniture with the portable power tools shown here.

Sectional Seating Units offer luxurious lounge seating in flexible form. Each light unit—they weigh less than twenty pounds apiece—is adaptable to make sectional sofas, as shown at right. They may also be used as floor seats, or mounted on various designs of chair platforms, as illustrated. Plans for making these platforms are detailed in the next chapter. For instructions on the upholstering of these units, turn to Chapter 8.

Furniture and interior designed by author

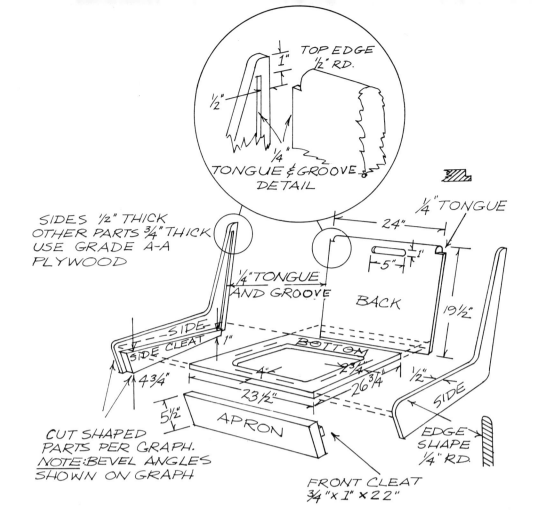

TOP EDGE ½" RD.

1"

½"

¼"

TONGUE & GROOVE DETAIL

SIDES ½" THICK
OTHER PARTS ¾" THICK
USE GRADE A-A
PLYWOOD

¼" TONGUE

24"

¼" TONGUE AND GROOVE

5"   1"

BACK

19½"

SIDE

SIDE CLEAT

1"

BOTTOM

4"   23¾"

½"

SIDE

1   4¾"

23½"   26¾

5½"

APRON

EDGE SHAPE ¼" RD.

CUT SHAPED
PARTS PER GRAPH.
NOTE: BEVEL ANGLES
SHOWN ON GRAPH

FRONT CLEAT
¾" x 1" x 22"

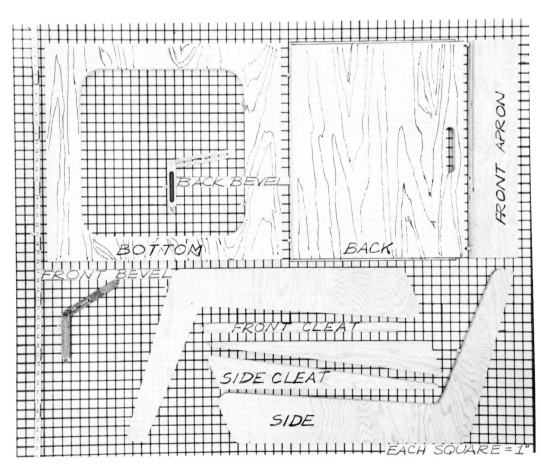

BACK BEVEL

BOTTOM

BACK

FRONT APRON

FRONT BEVEL

FRONT CLEAT

SIDE CLEAT

SIDE

EACH SQUARE = 1"

1 Side pattern is marked on plywood.

2 Saber Saw cuts sides to shape.

3 Belt Sander smooths edges of two side pieces.

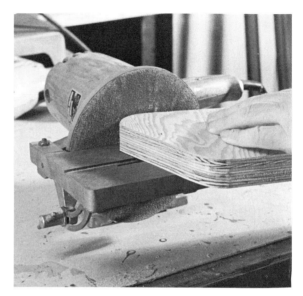

4 Disk Sander attachment of Power Unit smooths rounded corners.

5 Power Router shapes rounded edges.

6 Power Router cuts ¼″ groove for back panel.

7 Glue is applied to tapered side cleat and side.

8 Side cleats are clamped to sides.

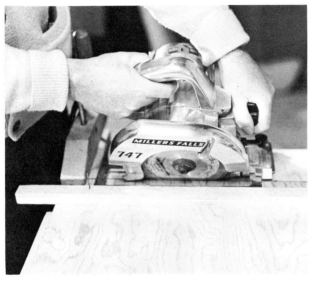

9 Circular Saw, guided by strip, saws end bevel of back panel.

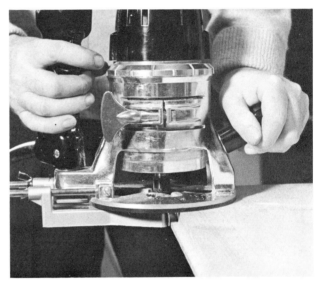

10 Power Router rabbets side edges of back panel.

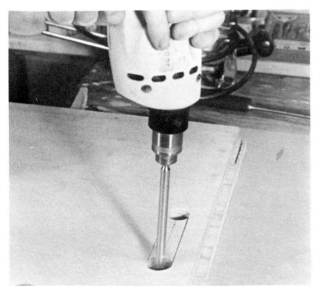

11 Electric Drill with ¾" high-speed bit bores ends of handle cutout.

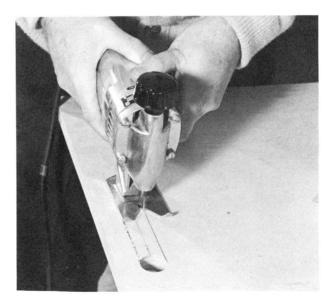

12 Saber Saw removes center portion of handle cutout.

13 Seat panel is cut out with Saber Saw. Inner edges are rounded with Power Router.

14 Circular Saw cuts beveled slots to receive "Elastic-Seat" resilient platform.

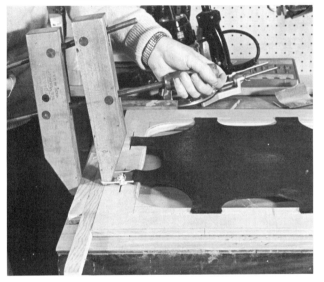

15 Beveled anchor tabs of "Elastic-Seat" platform are stretched into beveled slots.

16 Resilient platform and front apron are ready for assembly to back and sides.

17 Rabbet and groove joinery of back and sides is glued and clamped.

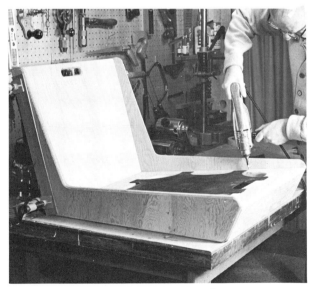

18 After glueing, Power Screwdriver secures seat screws to side cleats.

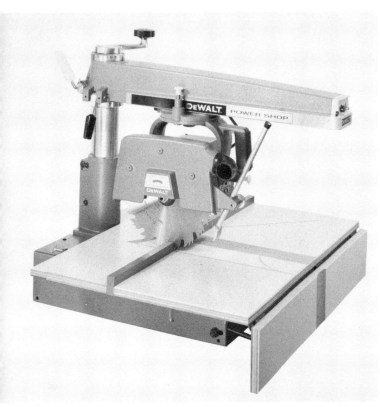

DeWalt Power Shop, Courtesy Black & Decker Mfg. Co.

HOW TO MAKE A "TUMBLE-TABLE" WITH WOODWORKING MACHINERY

Original design by author

If you are among those ambitious homecrafters who pursue woodworking for profitable production, you can increase your output with a combination woodworking machine like the Dewalt "Power Shop" shown on the facing page. With its many attachments this machine can build just about anything—and it performs with a maximum of speed and accuracy.

In cooperation with DeWalt, the "Tumble-Table" featured here, was built with this machine and photographed during construction. Since this involved cutting a variety of wood joints, as well as precise shaping of parts, the construction demonstrates versatility of this equipment. The operations photographed in the following step-by-step sequence also apply to the making of other projects with combination machinery. Of course, the convertible table can also be made with hand and portable power tools. But with woodworking machinery, you can do the job quickly and accurately.

Spacious coffee table, illustrated above, can be made either with veneered center panel as shown below or with leather or vinyl surfacing. (See Chapter 8.)

As illustrated below, this convertible table is "tumbled," on center hinges, from flat position as coffee table to upright position for dining or working.

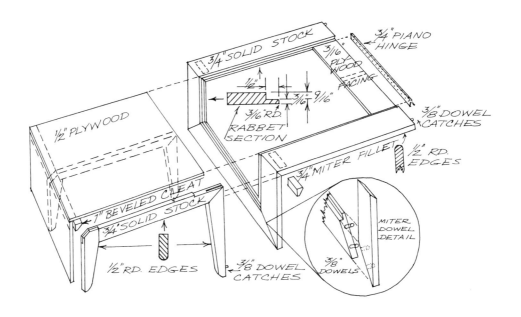

3/4" PIANO HINGE

3/4" SOLID STOCK

3/16" PLY WOOD FACING

1/2"

3/16" 9/16"

3/16" RD.

RABBET SECTION

3/8" DOWEL CATCHES

1/2 PLYWOOD

1/2" RD. EDGES

3/4" MITER FILLET

MITER DOWEL DETAIL

3/8" DOWELS

7" BEVELED CLEAT

3/4" SOLID STOCK

1/2" RD. EDGES

3/8 DOWEL CATCHES

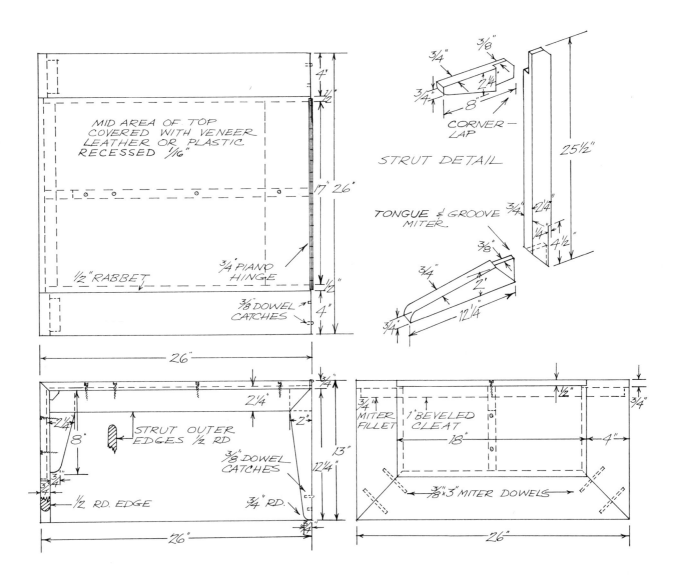

MID AREA OF TOP COVERED WITH VENEER LEATHER OR PLASTIC RECESSED 1/16"

4"

1/2

17" 26"

3/4" PIANO HINGE

1/2"

1/2" RABBET

3/8 DOWEL CATCHES

4"

26"

2 1/4"

3/4"

2"

8"

STRUT OUTER EDGES 1/2 RD

3/8" DOWEL CATCHES

2 1/4"

3/4"

4"

1/2 RD. EDGE

3/4" RD.

13"

12 1/4"

26"

3/8"

3/4"

3/4"

2 1/4"

8"

CORNER-LAP

STRUT DETAIL

TONGUE & GROOVE MITER

3/4"

2 1/4"

1/4"

4 1/2"

25 1/2"

3/8"

3/4"

2"

1/4

3/4"

12 1/4"

3/4" MITER FILLET

1" BEVELED CLEAT

1/2"

3/4"

18"

4"

3/8"x 3" MITER DOWELS

26"

62

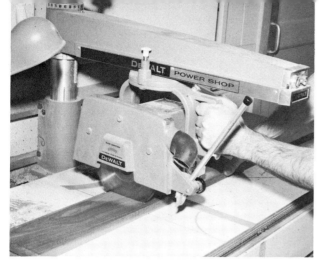

1 Lumber is crosscut to required lengths.

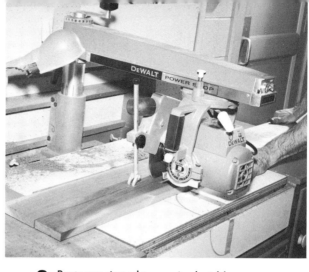

2 Parts are ripped to required widths.

3 Lumber and plywood parts, cut to required sizes, are ready for processing.

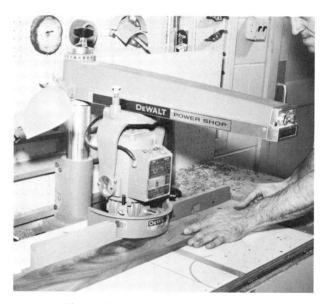

4 Shaper head, joints edges of frame and cuts rabbets.

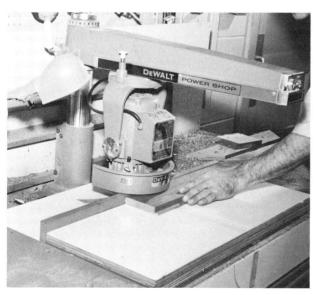

5 Rounded outer edges of frame are cut with shaper.

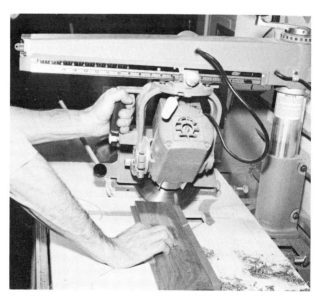

6 Saw is tilted for bevel cuts to miter top and end rails.

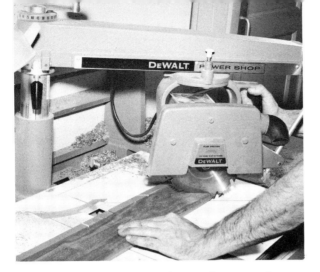

7 Saw arm is adjusted at 45 degree angle to cut face miters of end frames.

8 Dowel holes are drilled in end miters. Note use of guide jigs.

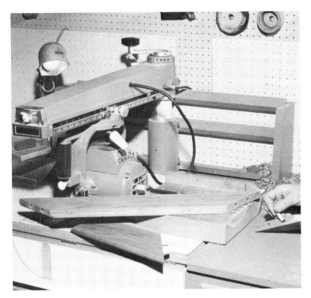

9 Dowels are glued in holes of one connecting miter bevel.

10 Doweled miter joint is glued, then pressed together and clamped in miter jig.

11 Mitered assembly of end frame is glued and clamped to top rails.

12 Bevel blocks, held with glue and brads, reinforce end miters.

13 Plywood center panel is assembled with screws and glue.

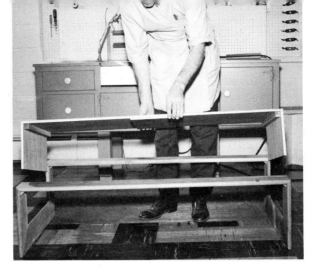

14 Center panel assembly is glued to rabbeted frame.

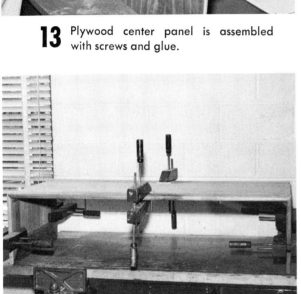

15 Glued assembly of center panels and frame is clamped to secure integral bonding.

16 Table is sawed in half at center.

17 Supporting struts are tongue mitered at one end.

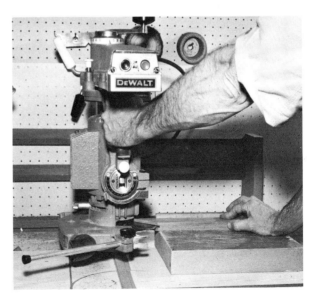

18 Connecting miter of strut is grooved for tongue and groove joint.

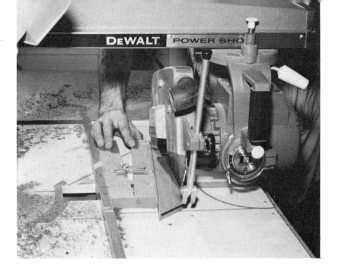

19 Adjustable jig guides tapered sawing of leg strut.

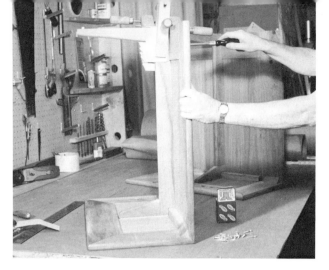

20 Assembly of truss struts is attached with glue and screws.

21 Screw indentations are plastic filled and sanded flush.

22 Piano hinge is attached to connect two halves of table.

23 Dowels, with sharpened ends, are glued in opposite legs to secure alignment.

24 Center panel is veneered or surface covered. (See Chapter 8.)

Photos courtesy DeWalt Division, Black & Decker Mfg. Co.

4

HOW TO CREATE CONTEMPORARY ROOMS

Furniture and interior designed by author

THE LIVING ROOM

Be a bit better than a woodworking duffer and you can create a bright, contemporary living room entirely on your own do-it-yourself plan. The accompanying illustrations show end and midway views of the same room to demonstrate what can be done. For all of this furniture was especially designed and built for this book—and there are no complications of construction. It will be noted the design of these pieces emphasizes modular flexibility. You can arrange them as you please, to suit your own decor. The sectional seating units, which are featured in step-by-step construction photos of Chapter 3, are used here to make the sofas and chairs detailed on following pages. Dramatic pole shelving applies interchangeably for both room divider and wall installation, offering numerous individual arrangements. Coffee tables come round and square, like the "Tumble-Table" shown at left (construction detailed in Chapter 3) and the spacious round-top, illustrated above. This, incidentally, can also be topped with a foam cushion to make the plump ottoman shown on page 74. Corner benches, with colorful foam cushions, are handy to have for additional seating, or, they may also be used as low tables for stereo and hi-fi. The pedestal chairside table is detailed on page 36. You will find the following pages describe each piece and give construction details. Related information on upholstering, covering and finishing is dealt with in Chapters 8 and 9.

SECTIONAL SOFA PLATFORMS

Sectional, upholstered seating units can be adapted to an almost unlimited variety of seating arrangements. The cozy corner assembly shown above is made with two platforms forming an "L." But the platforms can also be elongated to make sofas of any desired length or flanked to form "U" groupings. Build the platforms of flush doors. These can be purchased inexpensively in the stock widths specified on plan. If you don't mind an end overlap, you can use them, "as is" in stock lengths of 80″. But by following the shortening procedures, demonstrated on pages 38-39, the doors used here were cut down to lengths of 73½″ and 49½″, to form the "L." The shorter, two-place platform butts flush to the longer assembly. If you select doors with rich graining (mahogany and birch are most common), you may prefer to finish them naturally. Otherwise, paint your platforms to match plywood casings of the seating units. The units shown were upholstered with Du Pont derivative products—urethane foam and "Zepel" treated fabrics. Chapters 8 and 9 contain information on upholstering and finishing, applicable to this construction.

SOFA PLATFORM

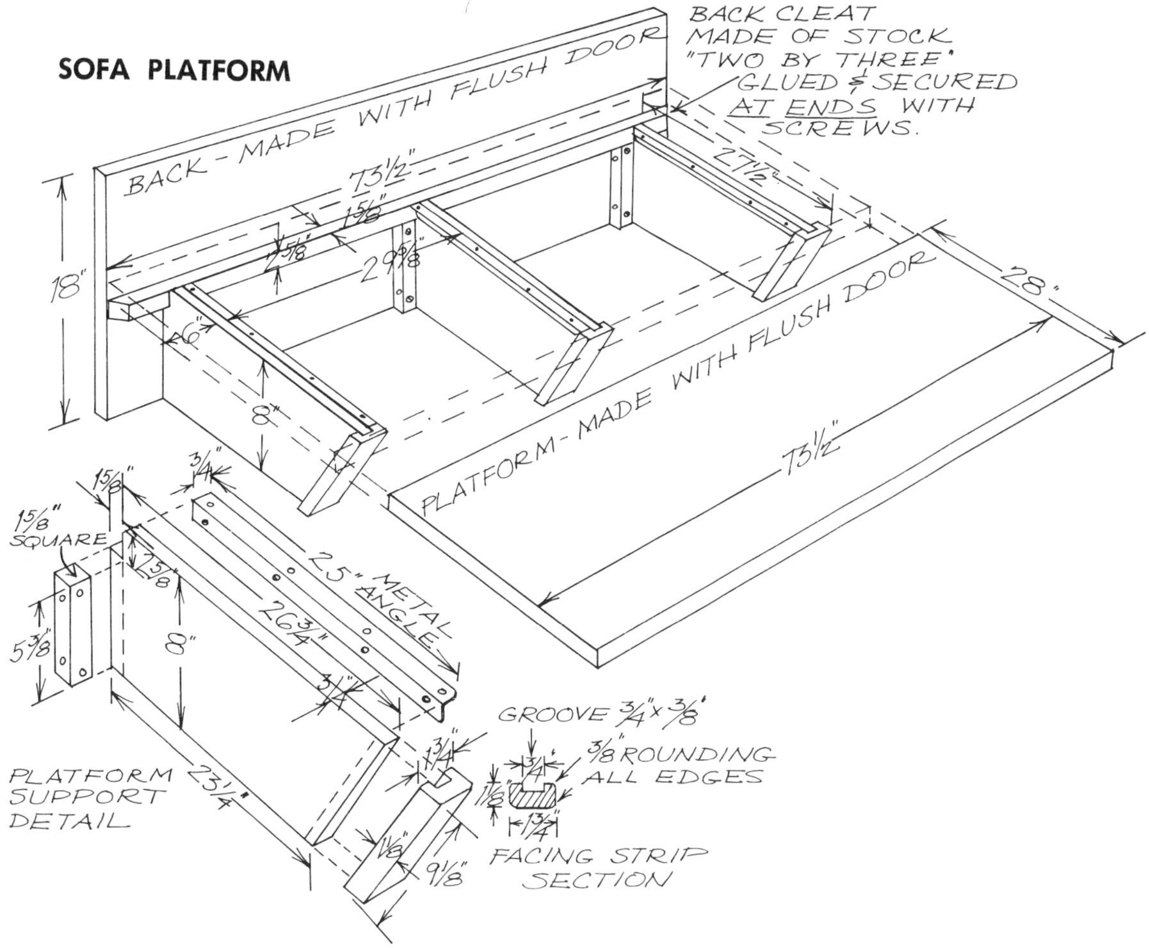
BACK CLEAT
MADE OF STOCK
"TWO BY THREE"
GLUED & SECURED
AT ENDS WITH
SCREWS.
BACK - MADE WITH FLUSH DOOR
73½"
27½"
1⅝"
1⅝"
29⅝"
18"
6"
8"
28"
PLATFORM - MADE WITH FLUSH DOOR
73½"
1⅝"
¾"
1⅝"
SQUARE
1⅝"
5⅜"
8"
25" METAL
ANGLE
26¾"
¾"
PLATFORM
SUPPORT
DETAIL
23¼"
1¾"
1⅛"
9⅛"
GROOVE ¾"x⅜"
⅜" ROUNDING
ALL EDGES
¾"
1⅛"
1¾"
FACING STRIP
SECTION

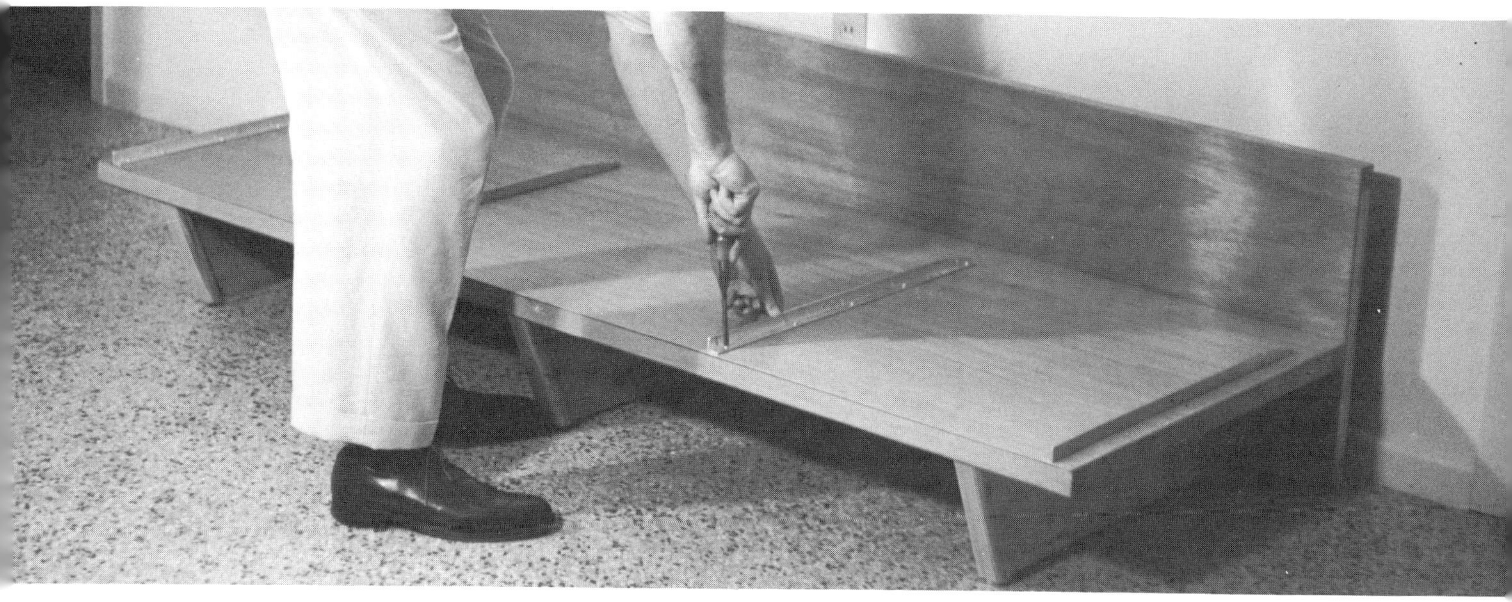

Metal angle strips, attached to surface of door platform, catch inner edges of seating units to prevent them from slipping around.

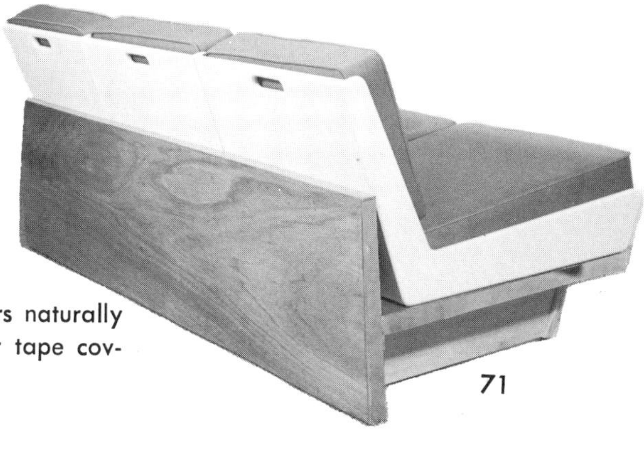

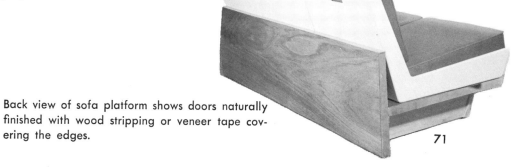

Back view of sofa platform shows doors naturally finished with wood stripping or veneer tape covering the edges.

SECTIONAL SEATING—
LOUNGE CHAIRS

Designs by author

The same sectional seating units, detailed in construction photographs of pages 54 to 59, implement design of the comfortable, contemporary lounge chairs illustrated on these pages. Again it is simply a matter of making platforms and armrest housings into which the units fit.

For the lighter "hairpin" chair platform, shown at the left, arm and leg members are cut integrally to dimensions of plan, from a panel of ¾″ plywood. Use of ordinary plywood presumes, however, that you intend to paint your parts. (If you prefer the natural graining of rich, solid woods, you will have to make each hairpin of 3 separate pieces joining them with dowels or lap joints, at the top.) The arms are foam upholstered, following procedures of page 170. They are attached with angle plates. To avoid an insecure assembly of parts, be sure the seat platform and spanning

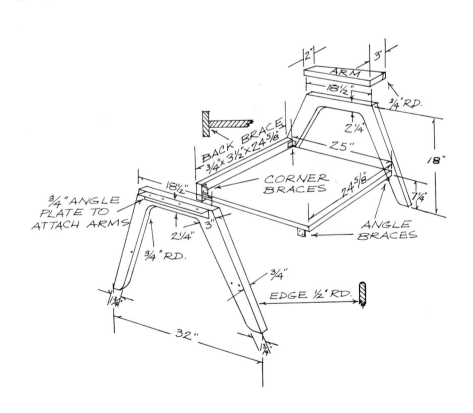

members are firmly attached to the legs. Use angle plates and 2″, #10, FH. screws, driven through the legs and into the edges of the platform, to reinforce this assembly.

The box housing for the lounge chair at the right is simply butted together of ¾″ plywood cut and shaped to dimensions shown on plan. If you have power equipment, you may prefer to rabbet the joints. For a strong job, use screws and glue to assemble your parts. Upholster the arms following procedures illustrated on page 170. The attachable 6″ Gerber legs fit flush to the corners of the base on slant adjustments.

If you make your chair housing of fir plywood, paint it an appropriate color. Otherwise it can be made of hardwood plywood of richer veneers and finished naturally. Or, you can cover the surface with fabric matching the upholstered cushions.

Designs by author

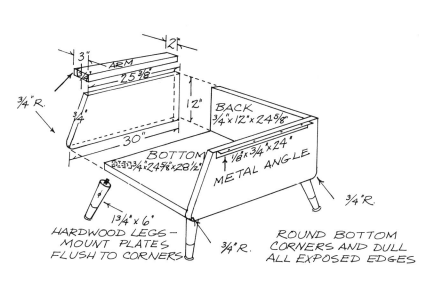

Design by author

COFFEE TABLE
AND OTTOMAN

Low furniture, of luxurious spread, adds convenience to contemporary living. When used as a coffee table, the simple design illustrated above, offers plenty of space for the magazines and accessories which generally collect around a sofa. However, it may also be fitted with a plump 4″ foam cushion to serve as a leg rest, or TV perch for the youngsters. In either capacity, its mobility is assured with 2″ ball casters. The simplicity of this contemporary design brings back the basics of cross-lap construction detailed on page 28. Armstrong vinyl was bonded to the plywood top surface of this model and the cross-lap base was made of white oak. Of course, you can use a variety of other contemporary woods. For information on covering and upholstering, refer to Chapter 8.

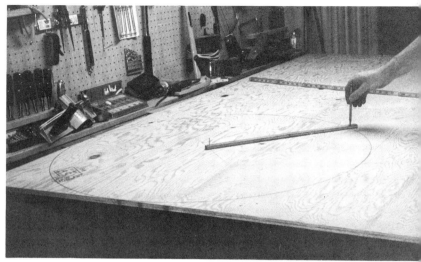

To make a perfect circle for the plywood top, drill two small holes at one-half the diameter on thin strip of wood. Pivot the strip at center and mark perimeter with pencil as shown at right.

Cross-lap base construction can be made even easier if end strips are omitted. Cross members are then cut to fit flush beneath edge of top.

COFFEE TABLE

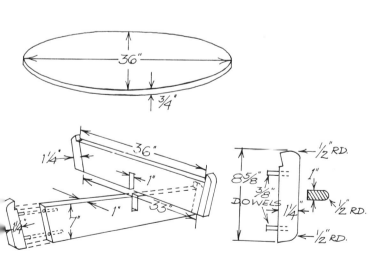

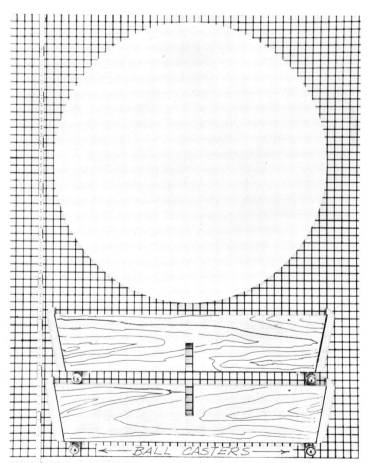

BALL CASTERS

SECTIONAL
BENCHES

Designs by author

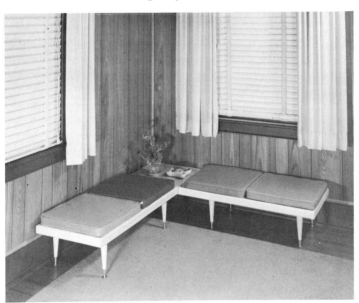

Probably no single category of contemporary furniture enjoys more widespread popularity than the assorted utility benches of recent design. A variety of these benches are presented in this book—some of them of rudimentary board construction, as shown on page 33. A clue to the ease of building them is the simplification of their separate, screw-on legs. These can be quickly attached to any surface to make benches, tables, chairs or stools. A really "custom-made" appearance characterizes sectional benches like those shown above, which demonstrate the beauty of natural wood graining with their laminated tops of fine veneer. Thus, as shown in plan, the ¼″ top panel is glued over a piece of ¾″ plywood. Rounded molding of matching wood then borders the edges. The result is a sturdy and rich looking bench which can be used with colorful, 2″ foam-filled pads for extra seating. Of course, these benches can also serve as coffee tables or they can be stretched along a wall for portable television, hi-fi or other equipment.

SECTIONAL BENCHES

NOTE: FOR LONGER BENCH
FOLLOW SAME CONSTRUCTION
BUT MAKE TOP 61" LONG WITH
ADDITIONAL 2 LEGS AT THE MIDDLE

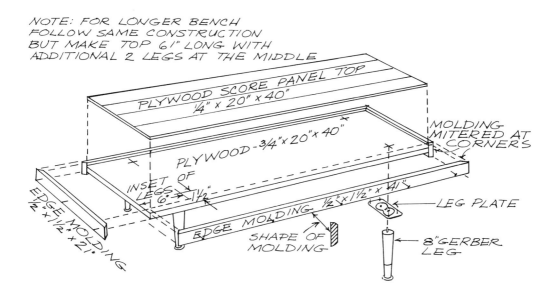

PLYWOOD SCORE PANEL TOP
1/4" x 20" x 40"

PLYWOOD - 3/4" x 20" x 40"

MOLDING
MITERED AT
CORNERS

INSET OF
LEGS
6" 1 1/2"

EDGE MOLDING 1/2" x 1/2" x 41"

EDGE MOLDING
1/2" x 1 1/2" x 21"

SHAPE OF
MOLDING

LEG PLATE

8" GERBER
LEG

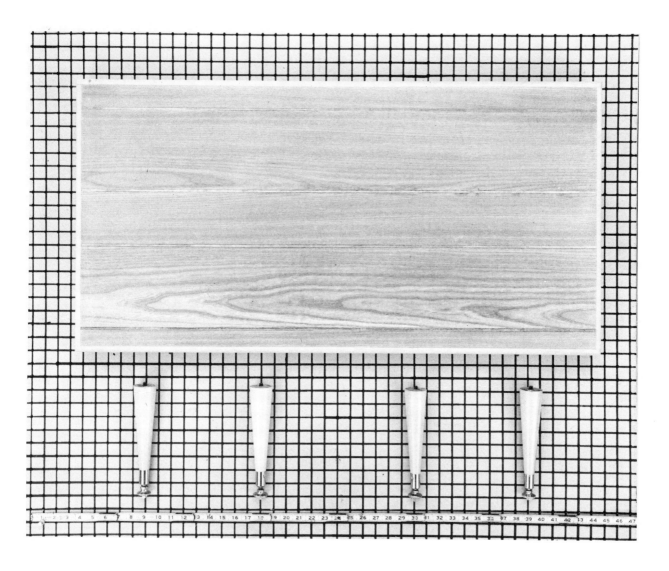

Indeed, you can become your own designer when you install sectional pole-systems. For they can be arranged any way you please; to stretch across entire walls, to bend around corners or to jut out from mid-areas to form room dividers. Moreover, they can be put up, taken down, and rearranged at any time to refresh your decor.

You need not be an expert to build your own pole-systems, and save money in the process. As detailed in the working drawing on the facing page, the systems illustrated require only stock materials. The poles are made of standard "two-by-threes" which cost less than one dollar apiece. Shelving is of plywood or seasoned lumber. You can even avoid the labor of boring the pole ends for the homemade dowel and spring details, if your hardware dealer stocks the spring-loaded tops which are now on the market. These spring-loaded caps fit over standard two-by-threes. With them it is only necessary to saw the standards to required lengths.

Designs by author

POLE SYSTEMS, WALL SHELVING AND ROOM DIVIDERS

Probably there's nothing more practical—nor more highly decorative in many individualized installations—than the various pole systems of contemporary furnishing, illustrated throughout this book. With the simple device of spring-loaded tension poles, which fit snugly between floor and ceiling, you can create the attractive shelving effects shown here. But this only offers a hint of greater possibilities—because you can amplify this arrangement with storage cabinets and various combinations of modular furniture also shown in Chapter 7 and elsewhere in this book.

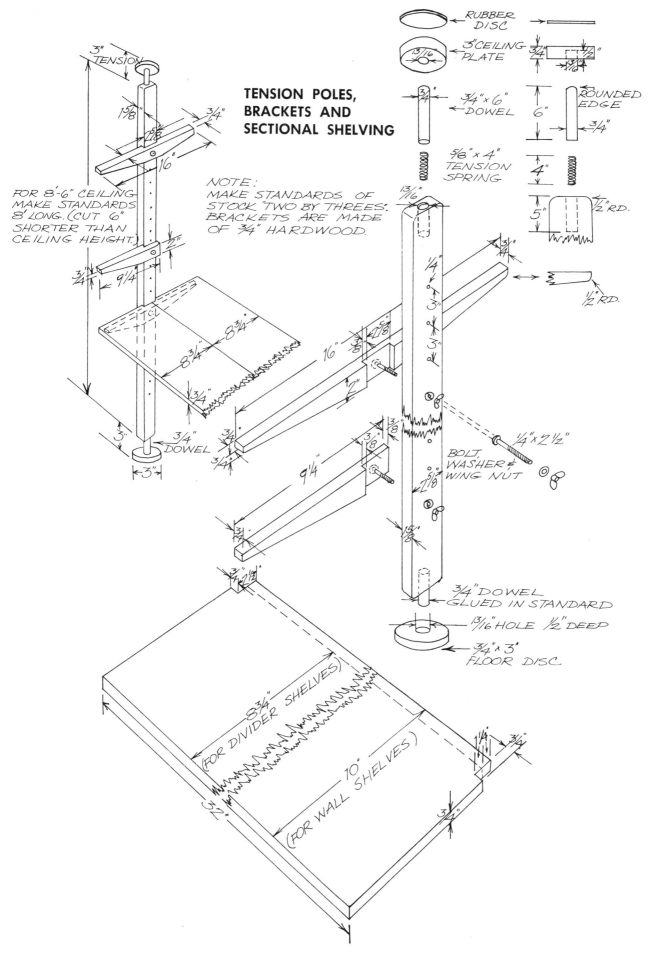

TENSION POLES, BRACKETS AND SECTIONAL SHELVING

3" TENSION

1⅝

2⅝

¾"

16"

FOR 8'-6" CEILING MAKE STANDARDS 8' LONG. (CUT 6" SHORTER THAN CEILING HEIGHT.)

2"

¾"

9¼"

8¾

8¾

¾"

3"

3"

¾" DOWEL

¾"

¾"

NOTE: MAKE STANDARDS OF STOCK "TWO BY THREES". BRACKETS ARE MADE OF ¾" HARDWOOD.

RUBBER DISC

13/16

3" CEILING PLATE

¾

½"

⅜/16

¾

3/4" x 6" DOWEL

6"

ROUNDED EDGE

¾"

⅝" x 4" TENSION SPRING

4"

5"

½" RD.

½" RD.

13/16

¼"

3"

3"

16"

1⅝

8

2"

¼" x 2½"

BOLT, WASHER & WING NUT

9¼"

⅜

8

2⅝

1⅝

2½"

¾"DOWEL GLUED IN STANDARD

13/16" HOLE ½" DEEP

¾" x 3" FLOOR DISC

8¾" (FOR DIVIDER SHELVES)

10" (FOR WALL SHELVES)

2"

¼"

¾"

¾"

THE DINING ROOM

The simplicity of clean lines, rich wood graining and complete practicality of function, distinguishes this contemporary dining room. The only overt embellishment comes from natural elements: woods, colorful fabrics, and accessories. This furniture blends into any setting and compliments any color scheme. You can build it yourself with the detailed plans which appear on following pages, or you can have it custom-built to these specifications. The handy homecrafter will not find any complications in this construction. Most of the parts are made of plywood. If a common type is used, the finished furniture should be painted. For the finest effect, however, these pieces should be made of hardwood plywood veneered with select woods of choice graining. The base of the table would then be made of matching solid lumber. All plywood edges must, of course, be covered with wood stripping or matching veneer tape when natural, grain finishes are desired. This furniture is particularly handsome when made of teak or walnut.

Furniture and interior designed by author

Natural graining of fine wood combines with colorful upholstering and choice accessories to create this cheerful, contemporary dining room. Chairs are foam upholstered with backs covered for bright effect. Side cabinets and drawer unit provide ample storage space for china, silverware and table linens. Top hutch unit, with paneled back, makes attractive setting for display of prized crockery and glass.

DINING-ROOM TABLE

You can build your own contemporary dining-room table by following construction details of working drawing on the facing page. For the average homecrafter who owns power tools, this construction is not difficult. In fact, the table can also be made entirely by hand, or you can substitute an even easier design of door-top table detailed in Chapter 2. It will be noted that the base is made of solid lumber, joined with dowels or mortise and tenons. Otherwise, the top is made of plywood panels with rounded molding, bordering the edges. As detailed on plan, this table is constructed of two separate halves. These may be stretched apart to receive a 24″ center leaf. This rests on metal flanges and is loose-doweled and secured with hooks and eyes. With insertion of the center leaf your table can be stretched to accommodate eight to ten people.

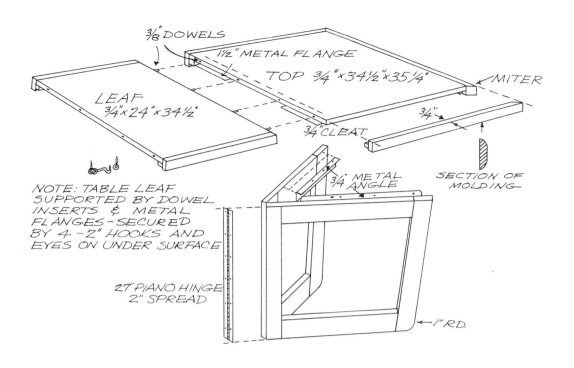

3/8" DOWELS

1½" METAL FLANGE

TOP 3/4"x34½"x35¼"

MITER

LEAF 3/4"x24"x34½"

3/4"

3/4" CLEAT

3/4" METAL ANGLE

SECTION OF MOLDING

NOTE: TABLE LEAF SUPPORTED BY DOWEL INSERTS & METAL FLANGES–SECURED BY 4–2" HOOKS AND EYES ON UNDER SURFACE

27" PIANO HINGE 2" SPREAD

1" RD.

DINING-ROOM TABLE

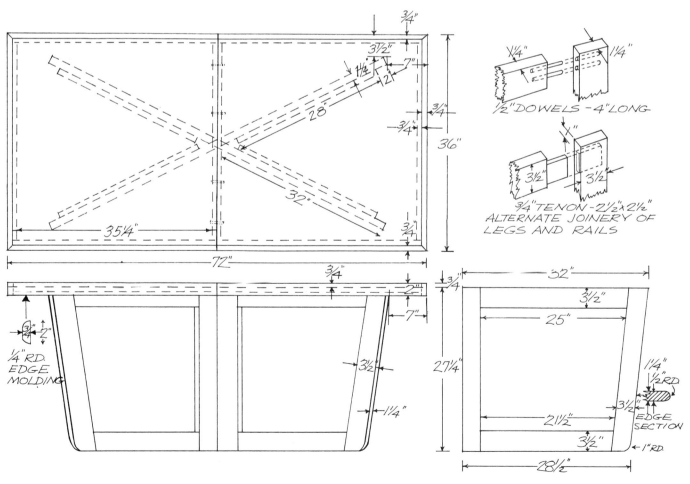

3/4"

3½"

7"

1¼"

2"

28"

3/4"

3/4"

36"

32"

35¼"

3/4"

72"

3/4"

2"

7"

3½"

1¼"

¼" RD. EDGE MOLDING

2"

1¼"

1¼"

½" DOWELS – 4" LONG

3½"

3½"

1"

3/4" TENON – 2½"x2½"
ALTERNATE JOINERY OF LEGS AND RAILS

3/4"

32"

3½"

25"

27¼"

21½"

3½"

3½"

28½"

1¼"

½" RD.

3½"

EDGE SECTION

1" RD.

Designs by author

SECTIONAL SIDE CABINETS AND CONTEMPORARY CHEST

The sectional side cabinets shown here are of simple box construction. They can be butt-fastened and joined with finishing nails and glue. (Of course, the more meticulous craftsman will insist on rabbeting or mitering the corners.) The door panels are fitted on Reynolds aluminum sliding door tracks. The center shelf rests on ¾″ aluminum angle brackets attached to sides. Whether you decide to paint, or prefer to finish your cabinet naturally to bring out grain patterns of richer woods, you should do the finishing before assembling the door panels. While you may only need one cabinet, you can save time at making two by following a sequence of sawing operations to cut duplicate parts.

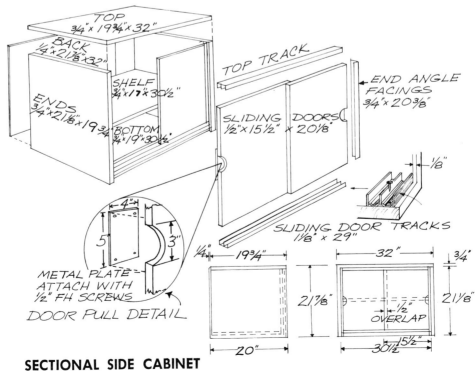

SECTIONAL SIDE CABINET

CONTEMPORARY CHEST

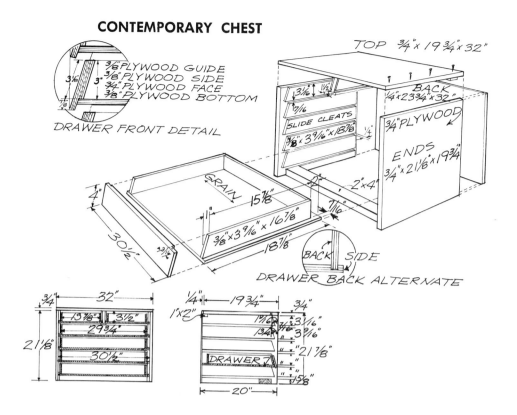

TOP ¾" x 19¾" x 32"

⅜" PLYWOOD GUIDE
⅜" PLYWOOD SIDE
¾" PLYWOOD FACE
⅜" PLYWOOD BOTTOM

DRAWER FRONT DETAIL

BACK ¼" x 23¾" x 32"

¾" PLYWOOD
ENDS ¾" x 21⅛" x 19¾"

SLIDE CLEATS
⅜" x 3 9/16" x 18⅞"

GRAIN 15⅞"

⅜" x 3 9/16" x 16⅞"

4"

30½"

18⅞"

2" x 4"

BACK   SIDE
DRAWER BACK ALTERNATE

32"

13⅞"   3½"
29¾"
30½"

21⅛"

19¾"
1" x 2"
3 1/16"
3 9/16"
21⅞"
DRAWER 7
15⅞"

20"

This chest of drawers departs from conventional construction. For the slanted drawer fronts have protruding bottom lips to serve as drawer pulls, thus eliminating the need of applied hardware. But there are other differences, too. The drawers are fitted together in box fashion, but with protruding plywood bottom panels. These slide into side grooves made by laminating a series of drawer separators inside the panels. Otherwise the casing is butted together, or, mitered at the corners, as your skill permits. For an especially attractive graining effect, saw all the drawer fronts from one panel of choice veneered plywood and rematch the graining when assembling the drawers.

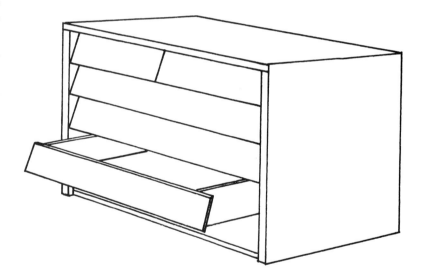

HUTCH AND BASE

Decorative aspects of contemporary furniture are enhanced by the display of things that go with it. Thus, the hutch illustrated above, while plain and simple of itself, becomes a handsome setting for the display of fine glass and dinnerware. And this design is simplicity itself to build. It requires little more than the skill of cutting the cross-lap joints demonstrated on page 28. This is best built of fine woods to match the chests and cabinets that go with it. Use random, plank-scored, ¼″ wall paneling for the back. If you have misgivings about cutting the end dados, simply eliminate them by butting and nailing the shelves flush against the ends.

The base is assembled of a standard, flush door of stock dimensions. To this a couple of cross cleats are glued and fastened with screws at the edges. The screw-on Gerber legs complete the leg assembly. Cabinet and drawer units should be secured to the base with a couple of ¼″ wing-bolts holding each unit.

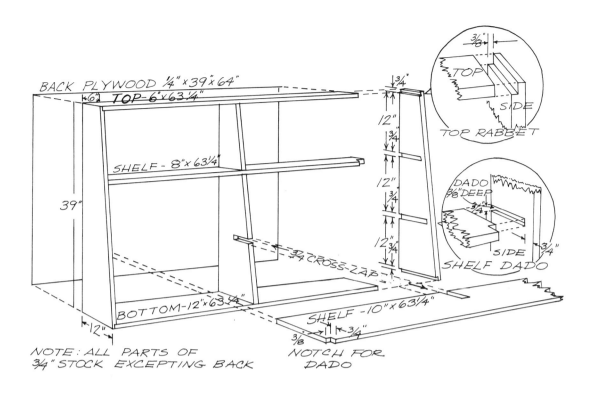

BACK PLYWOOD ¼" x 39" x 64"

6" TOP-6" x 63¼"

3/8"

3/4"

TOP

SIDE

TOP RABBET

12"

3/4"

SHELF - 8" x 63¼"

39"

12"

3/4"

DADO
3/8" DEEP

3/4"

SIDE

SHELF DADO

3/4"

3/4 CROSS-LAP

12"

3/4"

12"

BOTTOM-12" x 63¼"

SHELF -10" x 63¼"

3/4"

3/8

NOTCH FOR
DADO

12"

NOTE: ALL PARTS OF
3/4" STOCK EXCEPTING BACK

HUTCH

BASE

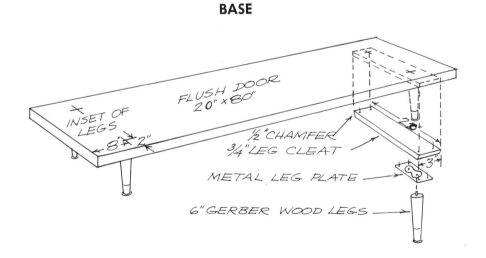

FLUSH DOOR
20" x 80"

INSET OF
LEGS

8" x 2"

½" CHAMFER

3/4" LEG CLEAT

METAL LEG PLATE

3"

6" GERBER WOOD LEGS

A CHOICE
OF CHAIRS

Designs by author

Side chairs, such as those illustrated, are not too difficult to build. The one featured at the right is made of plywood. This design goes with the contemporary dining group, already described. The seating parts are covered with du Pont derivative fabrics treated with "Zepel" for soil protection. Loose, urethane foam cushions assure seating comfort. Following similar seat construction, the pedestal based chair, in the middle, is the easiest to make. Plans for this chair appear on page 37. Somewhat more complicated is construction of the rope-wrapped chair, at the left. As the plan shows, this involves joinery of parts and some precision of fitting and shaping. But the nylon rope is easy to apply. You simply wrap the rope snugly in one direction and then cross-wrap.

SIDE CHAIR

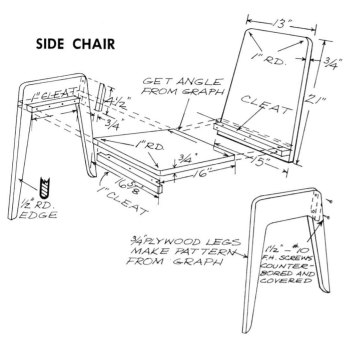

13"

1" RD.

GET ANGLE FROM GRAPH

3/4"

CLEAT

21"

1" CLEAT

4 1/2"

3/4"

1" RD.

3/4"

15"

16 5/8"

16"

1" CLEAT

1/2" RD. EDGE

3/4" PLYWOOD LEGS MAKE PATTERN FROM GRAPH

1 1/2" - #10 F.H. SCREWS COUNTERBORED AND COVERED

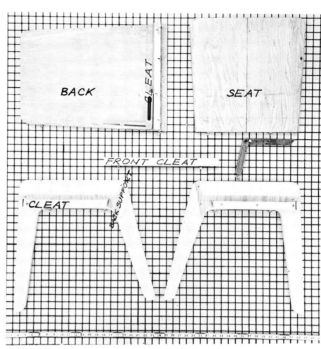

BACK

CLEAT

SEAT

FRONT CLEAT

CLEAT

BACK SUPPORT

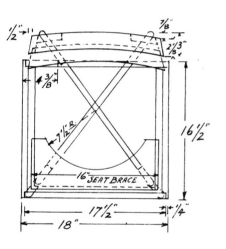

1/2" 1"

7/8"

2 3/8"

4 3/8"

16 1/2"

7 1/2" R

16" SEAT BRACE

17 1/2"

1/4"

18"

ROPE CHAIR

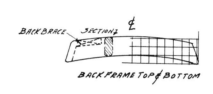

BACK BRACE   SECTION 2   ¢

BACK FRAME TOP & BOTTOM

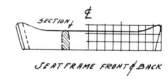

SECTION 1   ¢

SEAT FRAME FRONT & BACK

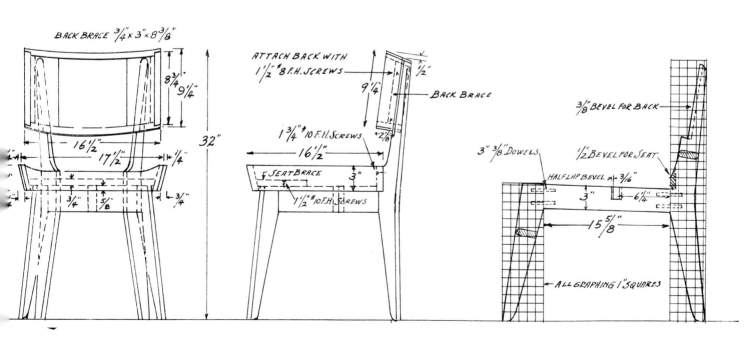

BACK BRACE 3/4" x 3" x 8 3/8"

8 3/4"

9 1/4"

32"

16 1/2"

17 1/2"

1 1/4"

3/4"

5/8"

3/4"

ATTACH BACK WITH 1 1/2" #8 F.H. SCREWS

1/2"

9 1/4"

BACK BRACE

2 3/8"

1 3/4" #10 F.H. SCREWS

16 1/2"

SEAT BRACE

3"

1 1/2" #10 F.H. SCREWS

3/8" BEVEL FOR BACK

3" 3/8" DOWELS

1/2" BEVEL FOR SEAT

HALF LAP BEVEL   3/16"

3"

6 1/4"

15 5/8"

ALL GRAPHING 1" SQUARES

89

WINDOW VALANCES

Window valances like those shown here are easily constructed over a base box of pine or similar soft wood. They are faced with ¼" veneer of prefinished paneling. Follow the construction drawing, butting the base parts together with 6-d finishing nails. The length of the valance is determined by the breadth of your windows. For a spacious effect, make them 12" longer than the spread of your window trim. This allows a 6" overlap for drapes on each side of the window. At your lumber dealer, you should be able to obtain remnants of prefinished paneling, veneered in woods to match your other furniture. As shown in plan, this is glued over the base construction.

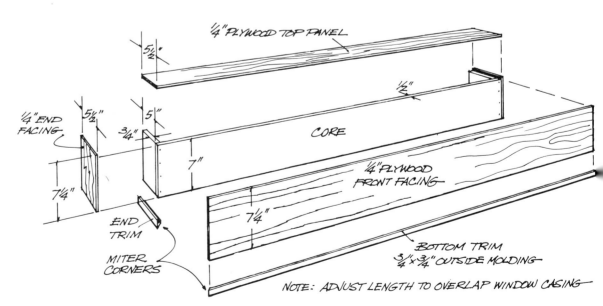

¼" PLYWOOD TOP PANEL

5½"

½"

¼" END FACING

5½"

¾"

5"

CORE

7"

¼" PLYWOOD FRONT FACING

7¼"

END TRIM

MITER CORNERS

7¼"

BOTTOM TRIM ¾" x ¾" OUTSIDE MOLDING

NOTE: ADJUST LENGTH TO OVERLAP WINDOW CASING

Furniture and interior designed by author

THE MASTER BEDROOM

Picture the bedroom, illustrated above, with all furniture components finished in rich grain tones of natural walnut or teak. Add tasteful colors for walls, deep-pile carpeting, bedspread, drapes and lamp shades. Then you will realize how the simple, unadorned lines of contemporary furniture contribute to the attractive decor and comfort of today's homes. For the furniture in this bedroom depends only on clean lines, good proportions and careful craftsmanship to express its appeal. Each piece shown here is easy to build— and can be made in your own choice of woods, to be painted or finished naturally. You can simplify the construction still further by making the bed headboard of a flush hardwood door, as described on page 41. The only item that could cause the amateur some construction trouble is the chest of drawers. So, if you are inexperienced and lack the proper tools, why not buy a couple of inexpensive, unfinished chests and finish them to your taste, matching the other furniture? Otherwise, by following the detailed plans of the next five pages you should be able to assemble this attractive furniture of your own do-it-yourself initiative.

Designs by author

The base illustrated, which accommodates two chests, is separately made to details of accompanying plan. It is attached with screws to chest bottoms. Following the same construction it can be shortened or stretched to accommodate one or more chests.

At your local glass dealer, you can have a plate glass mirror cut to dimensions of plan. The tapered frame should be made of solid wood. But for making the chest and base, use ordinary plywood if you intend to paint your finished products. Hardwood plywoods, of choice veneers, should be used if you want to bring out the rich graining effects of a natural finish. Of course, select grades of solid lumber can also be used if you have the skill and facilities for joining the boards.

SECTIONAL CHEST, MIRROR AND BASE

There's no need of ornamental hardware when you build this contemporary chest of drawers. For the slanted construction of drawer fronts provides an overlapping lip which serves as a drawer pull. Construction is further simplified with a series of drawer plates attached to the inner surfaces of the sides, with spaces between, which receive the protruding drawer bottoms. The drawers slide in the grooves thus constructed. Since these are sectional chest units, designed to fit end to end, you can make as many as you please. In fact, they are often constructed to fill entire wall areas.

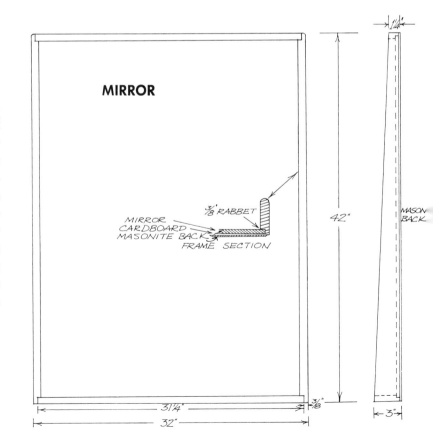

MIRROR

⅜" RABBET

MIRROR
CARDBOARD
MASONITE BACK
FRAME SECTION

42"

MASON
BACK

31¼"

⅜"

32"

3"

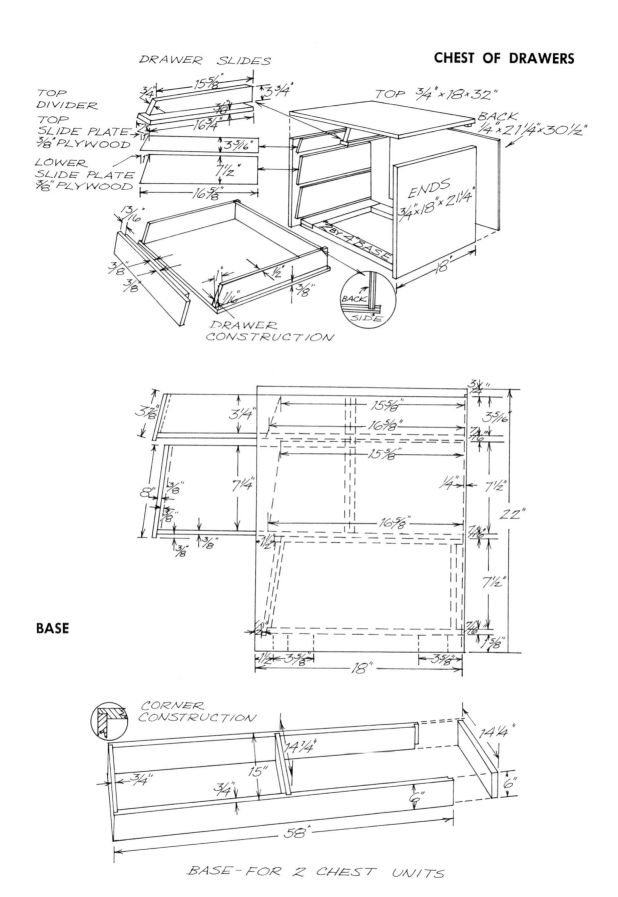

DRAWER SLIDES

TOP DIVIDER

TOP SLIDE PLATE ⅜" PLYWOOD

LOWER SLIDE PLATE ⅜" PLYWOOD

TOP ¾" × 18 × 32"

BACK ¼" × 21¼" × 30½"

ENDS ¾" × 18" × 21¼"

2 BY 4" BASE

BACK SIDE

DRAWER CONSTRUCTION

BASE

CORNER CONSTRUCTION

BASE—FOR 2 CHEST UNITS

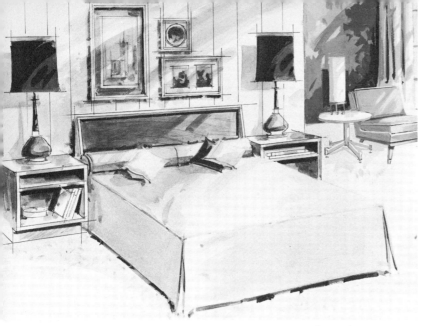

Hardwood plywood, veneered of choice woods, enhances the designs illustrated at left. Borders of headboard are made of solid, matching lumber. Exposed edges of consoles should be tape veneered or covered with matching strips of wood.

Designs by author

HEADBOARD

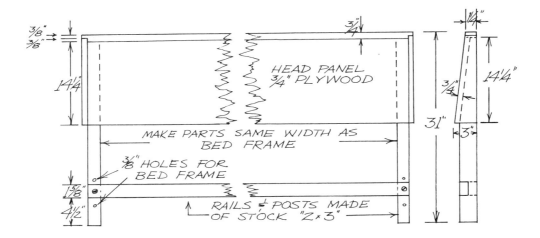

HEAD PANEL
3/4" PLYWOOD

MAKE PARTS SAME WIDTH AS
BED FRAME

3/8" HOLES FOR
BED FRAME

RAILS & POSTS MADE
OF STOCK "2x3"

HEADBOARD AND BEDSIDE CONSOLES

Certainly there's nothing easier to make than the headboard of a contemporary bed. You can even make one of a standard flush door as described on page 41. But the tapered styling of the design illustrated harmonizes with other furniture shown in this bedroom. Make it of a width to fit your box springs and mattress.

The bedside consoles are also easily butted together with plywood. They are pleasantly proportioned and provide ample top space and compartments for book, lamps and other bedside accessories.

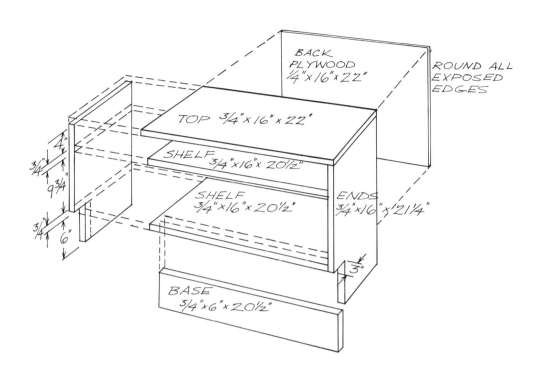

BACK
PLYWOOD
1/4"x16"x22"

ROUND ALL
EXPOSED
EDGES

TOP 3/4"x16"x22'

SHELF 3/4"x16"x20 1/2"

SHELF
3/4"x16"x20 1/2"

ENDS
3/4"x16"x21 1/4"

4"

3/4"

9 3/4"

3/4"

6"

3"

BASE
3/4"x6"x20 1/2"

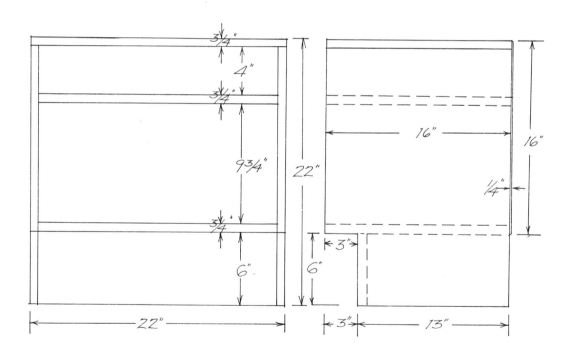

3/4"

4"

3/4"

9 3/4"

22"

3/4"

6"

22"

16"

16"

1/4"

3"

6"

3"

13"

Design by author

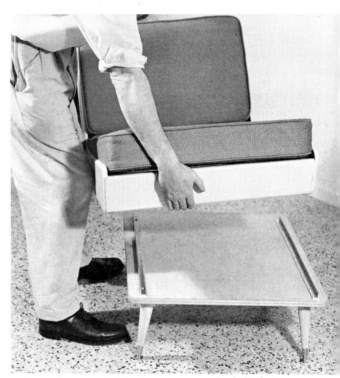

Plates for attachable legs are attached flush to corners of panel. Legs are screwed to alternate (slant) fitting of plate.

OCCASIONAL CHAIR

Once again, the sectional seating unit detailed in construction steps of Chapter 3, has been put to use to make an informal bedroom chair. This is its simplest application, because the platform on which it is mounted consists only of a piece of plywood to which 6" Gerber legs are attached. The little round-top pedestal table, shown beside the chair in top illustration, is put together of parts shown on page 36.

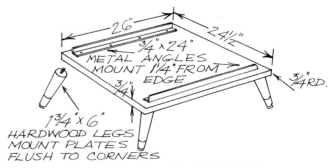

26"   24½"
¾"x24"
METAL ANGLES
MOUNT 1¼"FROM EDGE
¾"
¾"RD.
1¾"x6"
HARDWOOD LEGS
MOUNT PLATES
FLUSH TO CORNERS

CHAIR PLATFORM

5

CONTEMPORARY CLASSICS

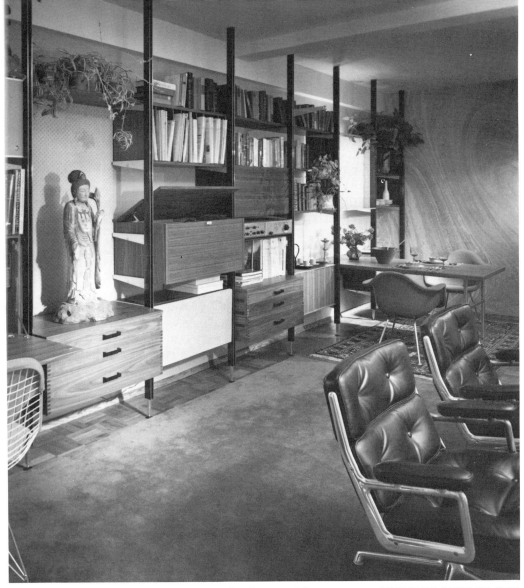

Designs by George Nelson; courtesy HERMAN MILLER INC.

CONTEMPORARY CLASSICS

This chapter focuses on the anatomy of distinctive American-made contemporary furniture. Starting with advanced concepts of modular sectional systems suitable for furnishing living areas, the following pages detail individual contemporary designs oriented to dining rooms and bedrooms. Like some centuries-old traditional pieces, these contemporaries are of such superb, functional design that they have become "classics" in their own time. The dimensioned drawings, which accompany the pictures, are not intended to suggest that it is easy for the amateur to reproduce this furniture. Indeed, it is not. But these drawings do show how good contemporary furniture is constructed. They show how parts are shaped, dimensioned and proportioned to obtain these professional results. Amateur craftsmen may gain by studying them—and skilled woodworkers should be able to reproduce them. It should be noted that some of these designs no longer form part of the product lines of manufacturers to whom they are credited. But this does not detract from their classical quality.

COMPREHENSIVE SECTIONAL SYSTEMS

Because they represent the most sophisticated and all-embracing development of the various sectional furniture systems shown in this book, the George Nelson Comprehensive Systems, pictured below and on the opposite page, deserve special attention. Mr. Nelson introduced an entirely new approach to the problem of furnishing the contemporary home. To accomplish this, he replaced scattered, free-standing furniture with an efficient and well-organized system of structural supports which carry any desired arrangements of shelves, cabinets, chests, desks, drawers, tables, sliding panels and other components. The installation can be planned to solve individual problems. Numerous combinations of components are available to enable the individual to organize his own arrangements.

As will be noted on the dimensioned drawings on the next page, dozens of different furniture units can be installed interchangeably on specially engineered aluminum standards. Each component has integral aluminum brackets for attachment to front or rear of the standards. Hardware is available in several types to make installation of poles practical in almost any situation. Wiring for accessory lighting units can be inconspicuously passed up through the poles at baseboard level. Measured drawings next page ▶

Designs by George Nelson; courtesy HERMAN MILLER, INC.

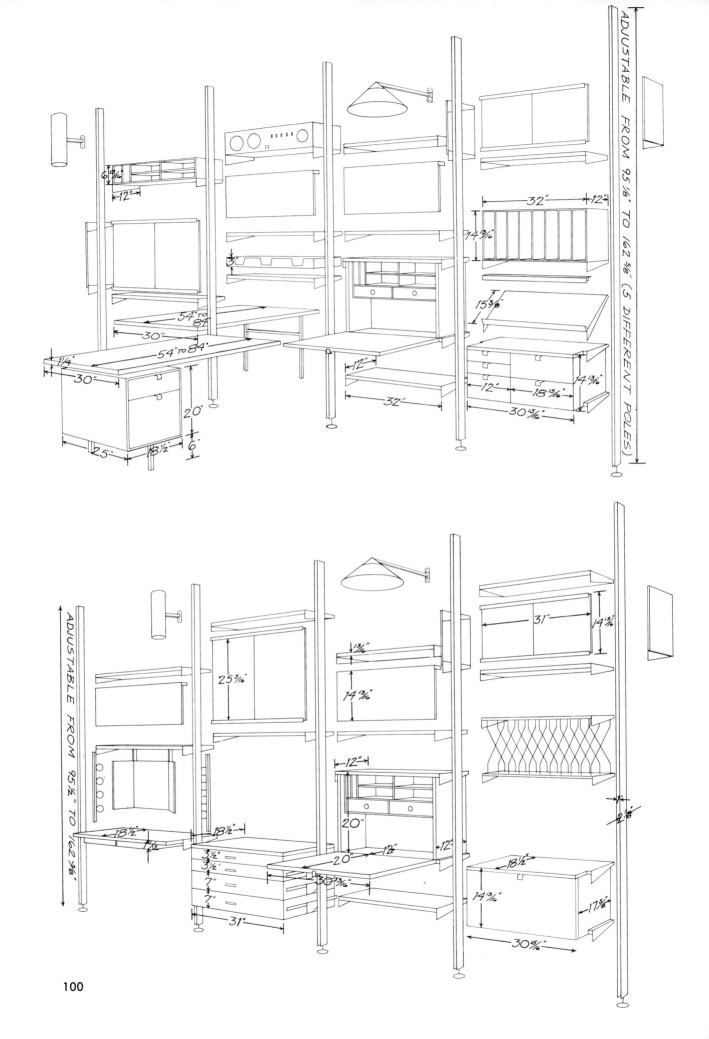

ADJUSTABLE FROM 95⅛" TO 162⅝" (5 DIFFERENT POLES)

6⁴⁄₁₆"
12"

32"   12"

14³⁄₁₆"

15³⁄₈"

54" TO 84"
30"
54" TO 84"
1¼"
30"
20"
6"
2.5"   18½"

12"   18¹⁵⁄₁₆"   14¹³⁄₁₆"

32"

30¹⁵⁄₁₆"

ADJUSTABLE FROM 95½" TO 162⅝"

31"   14¹³⁄₁₆"

13⁄₁₆"

25⁵⁄₁₆"

14¹³⁄₁₆"

12"

20"

18½"   18½"
½"

3½"
3½"
7"
7"

20"   12"

12"

1"
2⅛"

18½"

14¹³⁄₁₆"
17⁵⁄₈"

31"

30¹³⁄₁₆"

30¹⁵⁄₁₆"

CONTEMPORARY DINING ROOM

Clean, crisp lines—a fine feeling for the strength and grace of solid hardwoods—simple and natural design; all of these qualities make contemporary furniture uniquely at home for today's living. In the dining room, pictured above, sleek little sculptured chairs go with a striking buffet and glass-fronted hutch which provides a maximum of storage in a minimum of floor space.

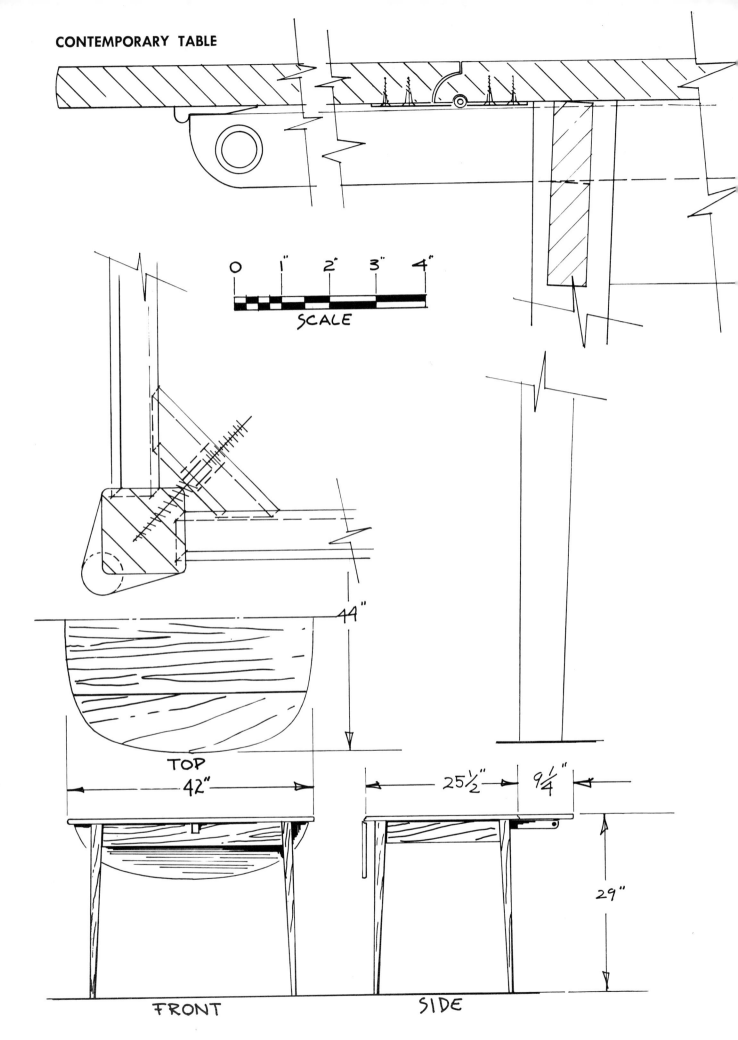

CONTEMPORARY TABLE

SCALE

0   1"   2"   3"   4"

44"

TOP
42"

25½"   9¼"

29"

FRONT   SIDE

Courtesy of HEYWOOD-WAKEFIELD COMPANY

CONTEMPORARY TABLE

The dining table, designed by W. Joseph Carr, is of subtle proportions and maintains a disarming simplicity of style in harmony with the group pictured on the previous page. This graceful little table has drop leaves and can be placed against a wall, if desired.

Design by Leo Siranek; courtesy HEYWOOD-WAKEFIELD COMPANY

SIDE CHAIR

If this was not an entirely original design by Leo Siranek, its simplicity of form and solid-wood construction would identify it with some of the provincial chair designs which originated in Europe, over a century ago. But a glance at the accompanying working drawing reveals that there's considerable subtlety to the achievement of such simplicity. Note the angling, tapering and proportioning of parts and the sculptured shaping of the curved back. All of these details demonstrate that the creation of simple effects in contemporary chair design is not always accomplished with an equally simple assembly of parts.

SIDE CHAIR

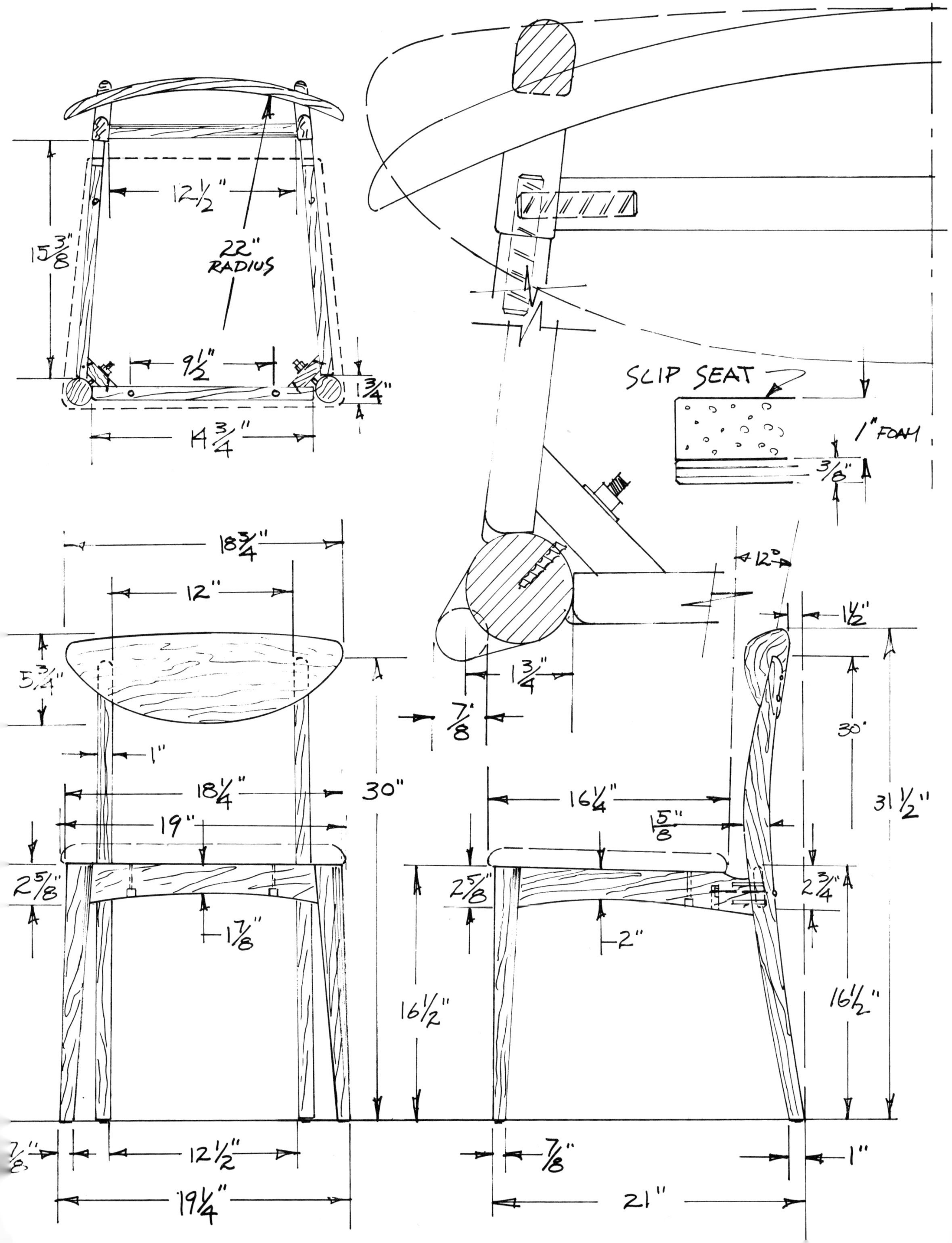

12½"

15⅜"

22" RADIUS

9½"

¾"

14¾"

SLIP SEAT

1" FOAM

⅜"

18¾"

12"

5¾"

1"

18¼"

30"

19"

2⅝"

1⅞"

16½"

7⅛"

12½"

19¼"

12°

1½"

30"

16¼"

⅝"

31½"

2⅝"

2"

2¾"

16½"

1¾"

⅞"

⅞"

21"

1"

Design by W. Joseph Carr; courtesy HEYWOOD-WAKEFIELD COMPANY

CONTEMPORARY BUFFET
AND CHINA HUTCH

The contemporary buffet and china hutch, by W. Joseph Carr, almost conveys an "early American" simplicity of design. But since it avoids all pretense of embellishment in the way of scrollwork, its appeal is made with fine balance and proportioning of parts. Then, too, by adhering to that tenet of contemporary design which prescribes that all adornment should be natural, the buffet and hutch are dressed in the beauty of natural wood graining and ornamented by a decorative display of china and accessories. As will be noted, the hutch is fronted with glass panel doors which protect the china and accent its display.

CONTEMPORARY BUFFET

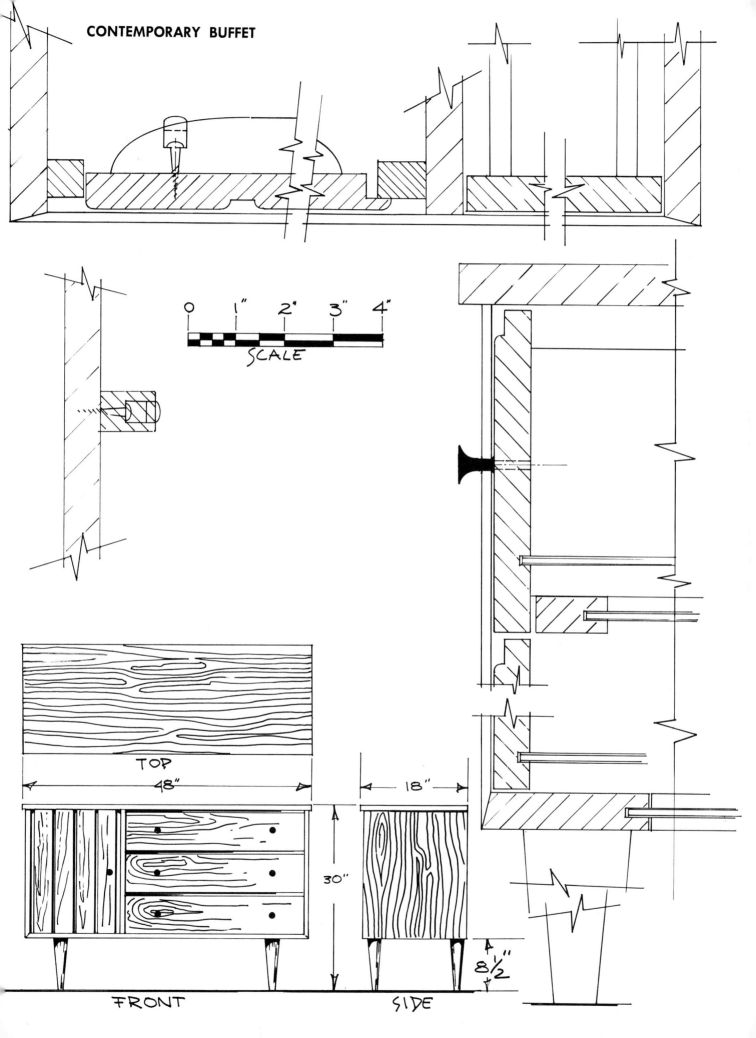

SCALE

0   1"   2"   3"   4"

TOP

48"

30"

8½"

FRONT

18"

SIDE

CHINA HUTCH

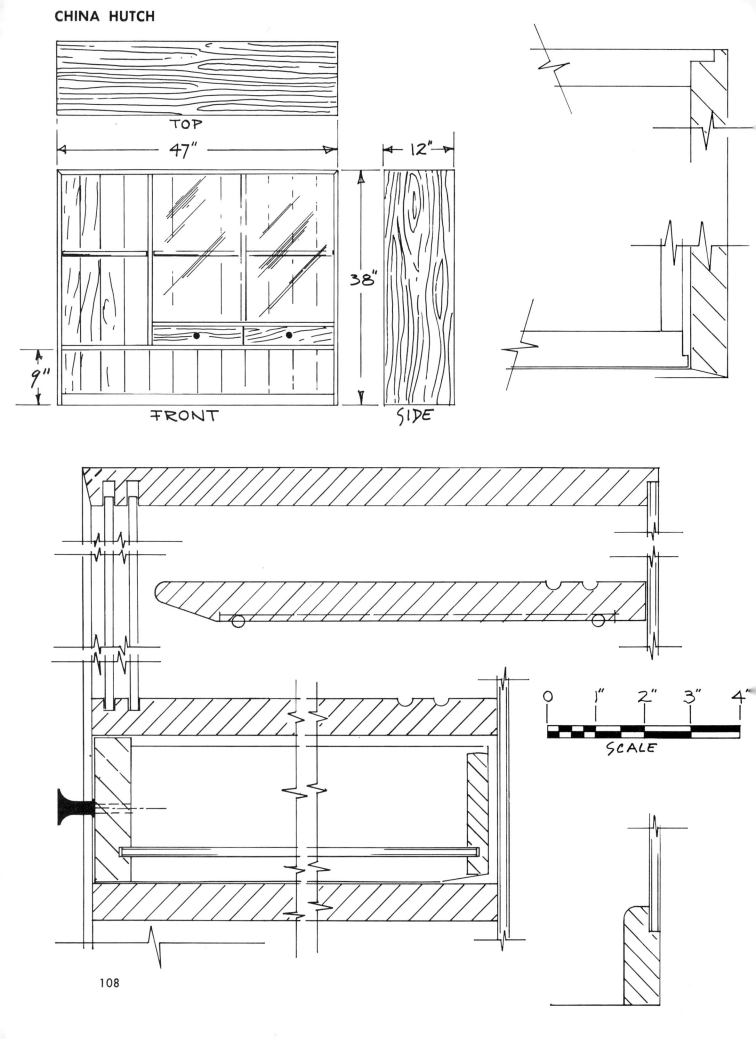

TOP

47"

12"

38"

9"

FRONT

SIDE

0   1"   2"   3"   4"

SCALE

108

Courtesy of HEYWOOD-WAKEFIELD COMPANY

CONTEMPORARY BEDROOM

Solid ash wood, seasoned and crafted under controlled conditions, was used to make the contemporary bedroom collection pictured above. Each piece is hand finished to bring out the mellow tones of natural wood graining. While simplicity keynotes all designs, pleasing effects have been produced in the shaping of base parts and integral drawer pulls. This furniture satisfies the need for ample storage and at the same time creates a neat, uncluttered appearance. It is easy to clean and reduces housekeeping chores to a minimum.

Design by Jan Knudsen; courtesy HEYWOOD-WAKEFIELD COMPANY

DOUBLE DRESSER AND MIRROR

The functional efficiency of contemporary furniture is produced with precise engineering of all parts. The drawers of the double dresser, pictured above, slide on metal glides for complete ease of movement. Tops of laminated plastic reflect rich wood graining corresponding to other parts but offer lasting surface protection and can be wiped clean in a jiffy. These designs express themselves in unostentatious virility of line which creates a natural organic composition. Thus they have the functional beauty of something alive. Ornamentation is obtained with accessories—lamps, flowers and the symmetrically shaped mirror detailed on page 112.

DOUBLE DRESSER

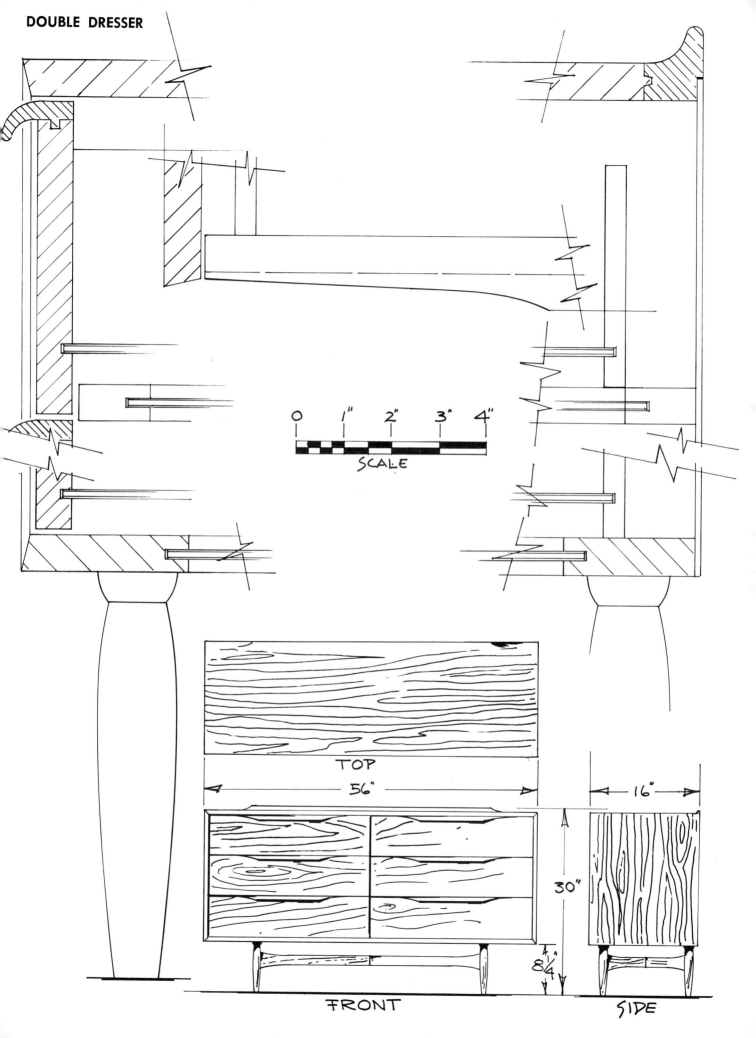

0 1" 2" 3" 4"

SCALE

TOP

56"

16"

30"

8¼"

FRONT

SIDE

MIRROR FRAME

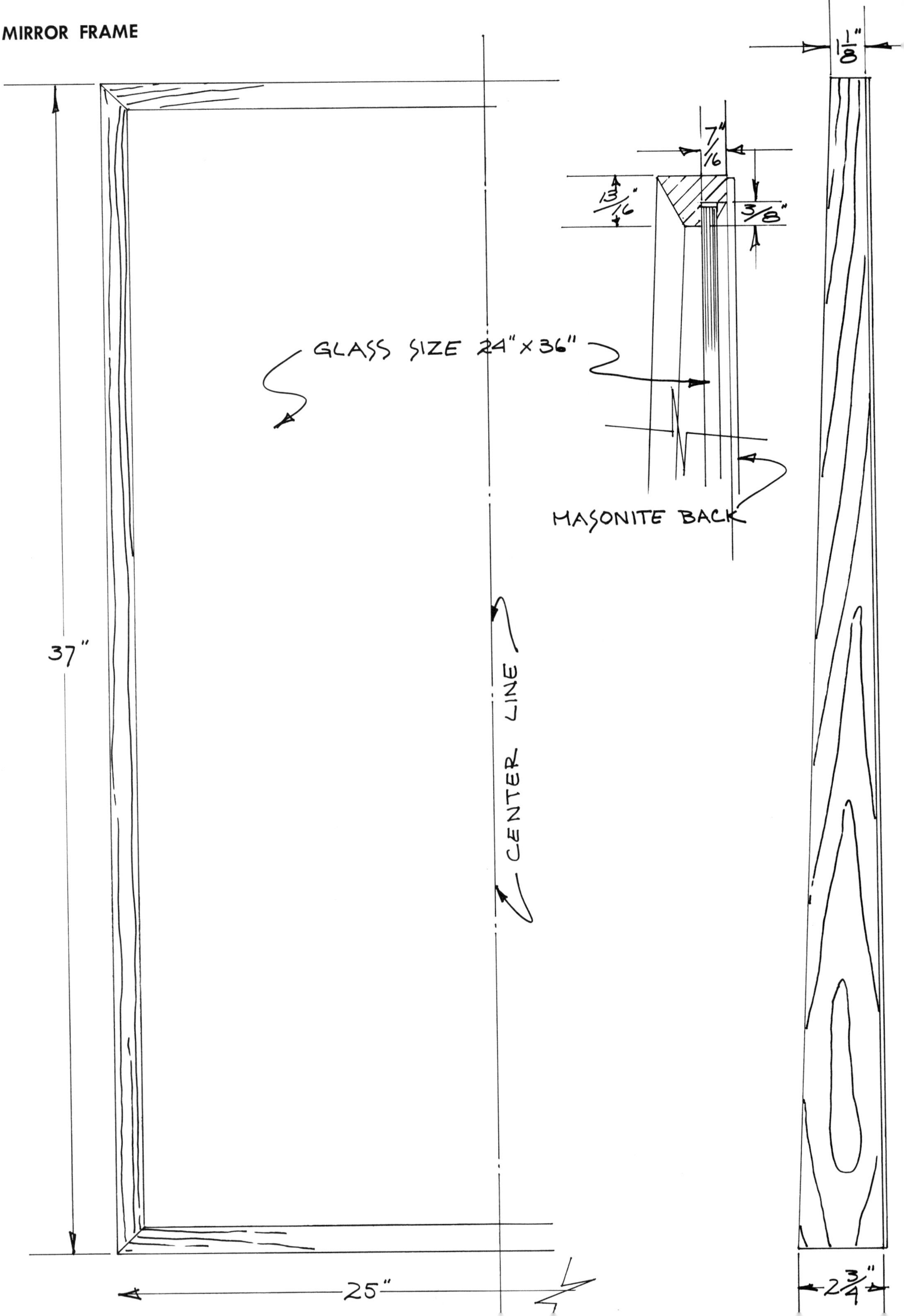

GLASS SIZE 24" X 36"

MASONITE BACK

37"

CENTER LINE

25"

1/8"

7/16"

13/16"

3/8"

2 3/4"

Design by Jan Knudsen; courtesy HEYWOOD-WAKEFIELD COMPANY

CHEST

Serving as a companion piece to the double dresser illustrated on previous pages, the five-drawer chest offers the advantage of ample drawer space housed in a contemporary chest of fine proportions and design. The top surface is plastic laminated for protection. Drawers glide in and out at the touch of a fingertip on specially engineered metal slides. Made of solid wood which has been scientifically processed, beautifully crafted and hand finished, contemporary furniture of this character offers lifetime durability plus the ultimate of functional efficiency.

Measured drawing next page ▶

FIVE-DRAWER CHEST

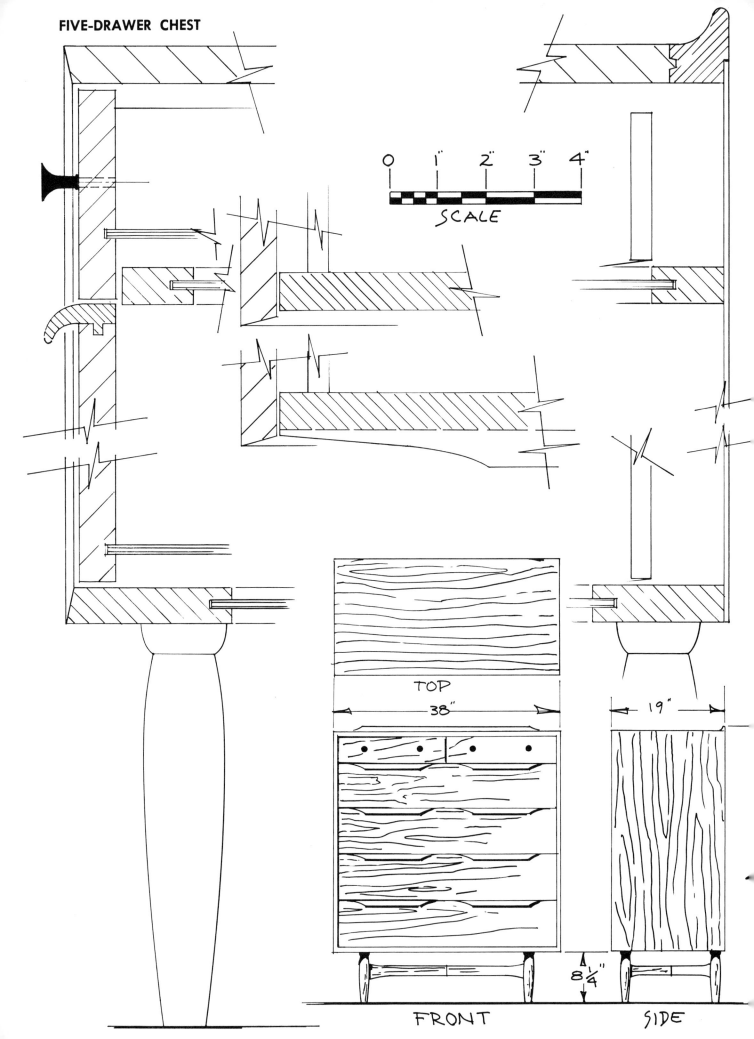

SCALE

0 1" 2" 3" 4"

TOP

38"

19"

8 1/4"

FRONT

SIDE

Design by W. Joseph Carr; courtesy HEYWOOD-WAKEFIELD COMPANY

BED

Contemporary beds are essentially simple, consisting usually of a paneled headboard attached to the metal bed frame which supports box springs and mattress. Since the metal frame can be purchased independently, for various standard sizes of springs, the headboard must only conform to the width of the frame. The one illustrated consists merely of a solid-wood panel mounted on two standards. But there is some subtlety to the shaping and finishing of these parts. Fine, natural wood graining enriches the surface and all edges are rounded to shape shown on plan. Measured drawing next page ▶

BED HEADBOARD

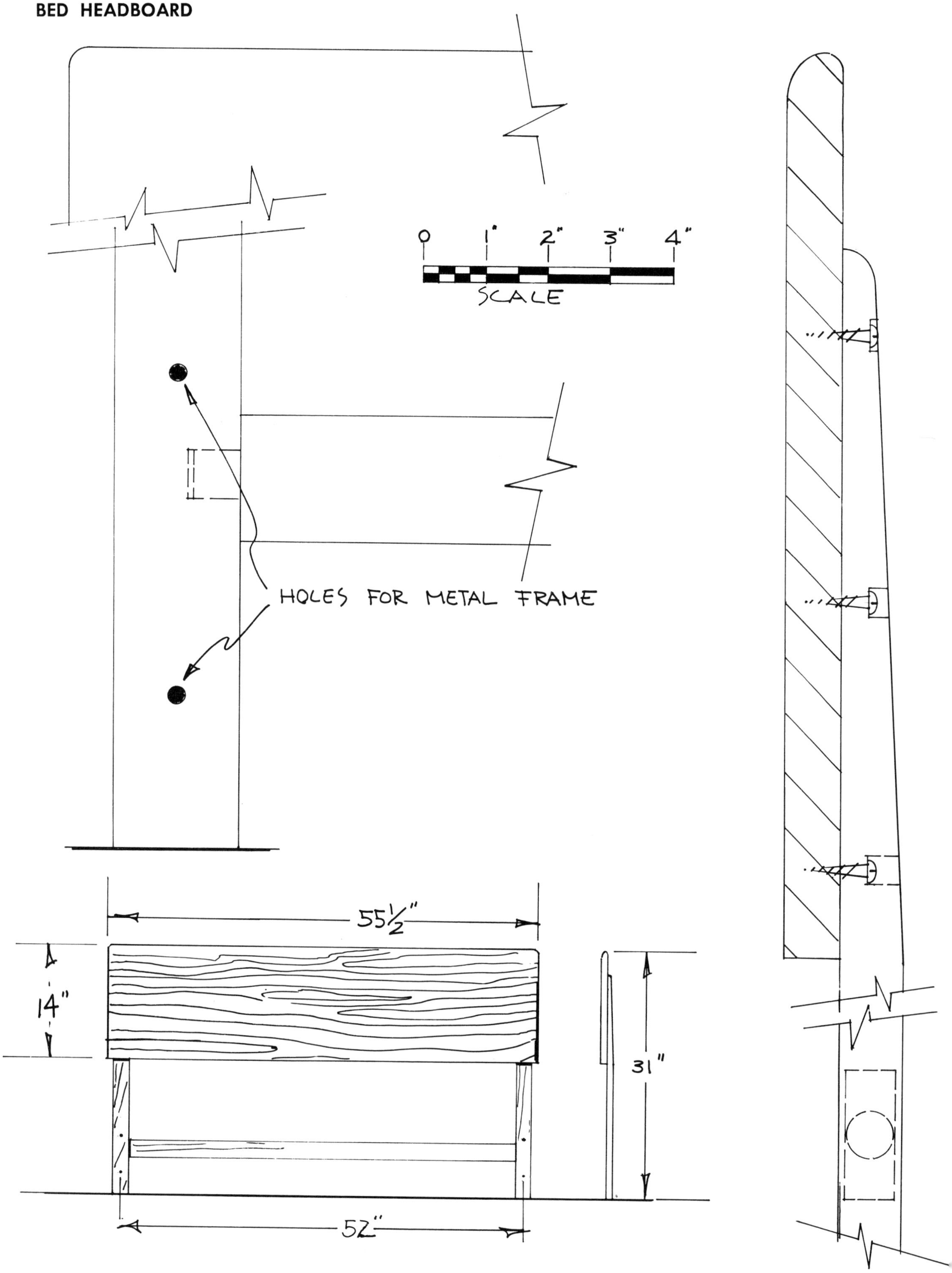

0   1"   2"   3"   4"

SCALE

HOLES FOR METAL FRAME

55½"

14"

31"

52"

Design by Jan Knudsen; courtesy HEYWOOD-WAKEFIELD COMPANY

NIGHT TABLE

This crafty console provides ample room beside the bed for lamp, telephone, radio, books, magazines, papers and all other items which are nice to have at hand during hours of relaxation. It is a pleasant little design in itself and may be equally at home beside a chair or sofa. Made of solid wood and finished naturally, this little cabinet-table is beautifully designed and proportioned to do its job. The top is plastic laminated to protect the surface. The front of the drawer overlaps to provide a continuous drawer-pull. This makes it easy to slide the drawer in or out from a side position while lying on the bed.

Measured drawing next page ▶

NIGHT TABLE

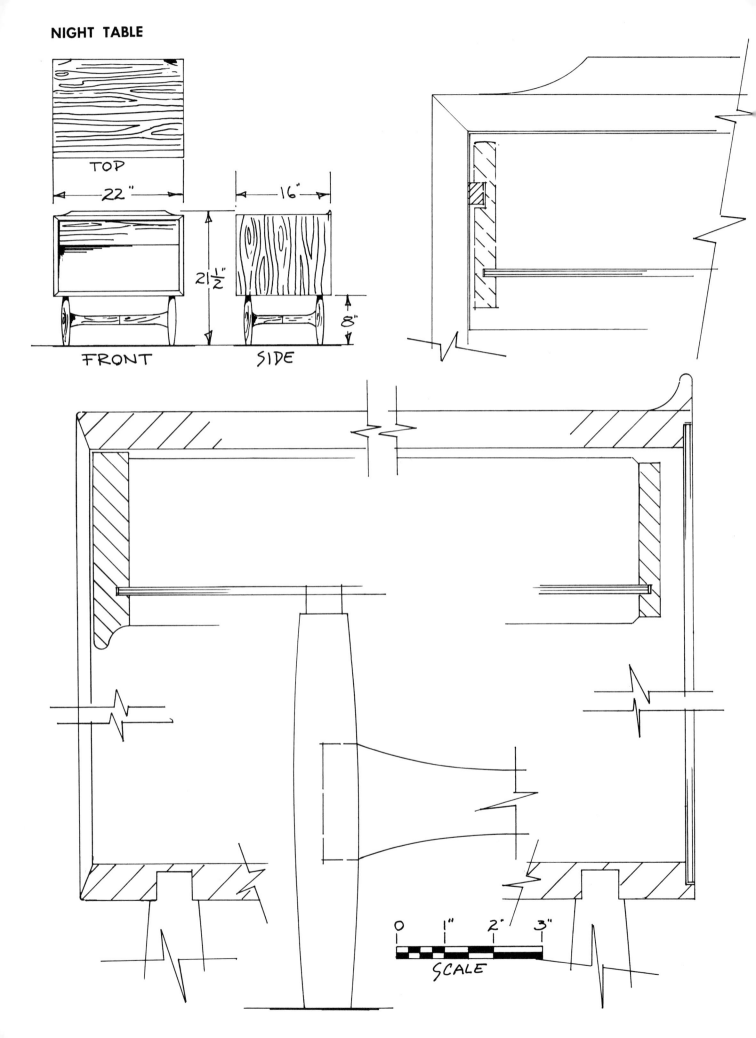

TOP

22"

FRONT

SIDE

21½"

16"

8"

0 1" 2" 3"

SCALE

Design by W. Joseph Carr; courtesy HEYWOOD-WAKEFIELD COMPANY

LOUNGE CHAIR

New techniques of upholstering have brought about drastic improvements in the design of soft seating. Taking advantage of technical progress in the manufacture of foam cushioning and resilient new seat platforms (of strap webbing or elastic stretch materials) contemporary designers now produce lounge chairs and sofas of extreme comfort but with only a fraction of the weight of the old-fashioned spring-platform, burlap and bulk-padded upholstery. An example of this is the light-weight contemporary lounge chair, illustrated above. Upholstered with reinforced rubber-strap platforms for resilient support of foam-filled, sectional seat and back cushions, this chair is properly contoured for perfect comfort. Even the top section of the reversible foam back cushion is tilted forward at a slight angle to act as a head rest. The companion leg rest is similarly upholstered, thus providing an attractive combination for complete, stretch-out relaxation.

Measured drawing next page ▶

LOUNGE CHAIR

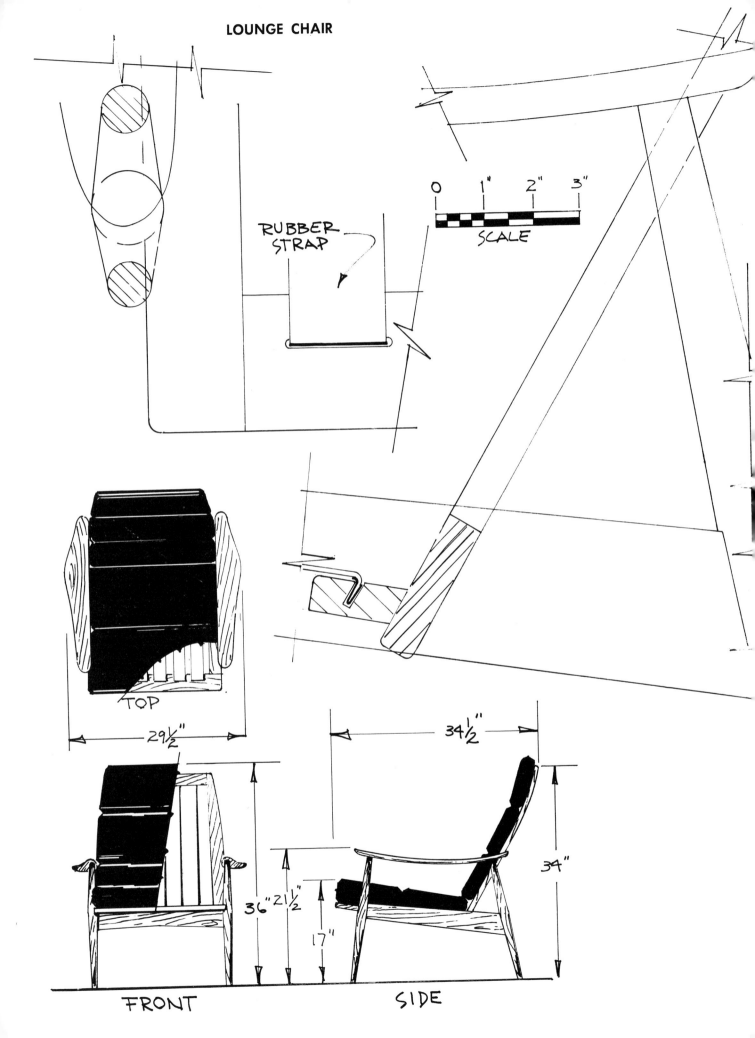

RUBBER
STRAP

0   1"   2"   3"
SCALE

TOP

29½"

FRONT

34½"

36" 21½"

17"

34"

SIDE

Design by W. Joseph Carr; courtesy HEYWOOD-WAKEFIELD COMPANY

LEG REST

Even the simplest objects of contemporary design emerge as items of sculptured elegance when carefully crafted to the designer's exacting specifications. As an example, the little leg rest—fashioned to complement the lounge chair previously illustrated—has all the functional attributes of its companion piece. It is foam-upholstered and can be used separately (especially by young TV-watchers) as a useful addition to the furnishing of any contemporary room. Measured drawing next page ▶

LEG REST

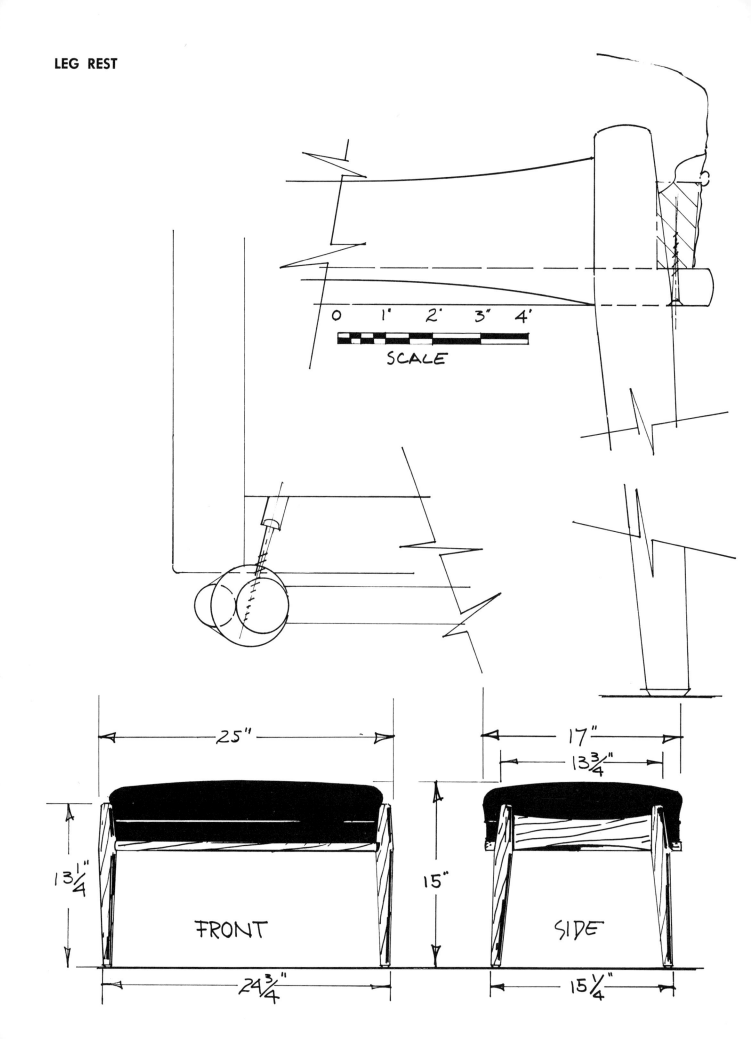

0   1'   2'   3"   4'

SCALE

25"

17"

13¾"

13¼"

15"

FRONT

SIDE

24¾"

15¼"

6
CONTEMPORARY BUILT-INS

Designs by Don Blair; courtesy Western Wood Products Association

CONTEMPORARY BUILT-INS

By taking on the appearance of being an integral part of the room, built-in furniture contributes to the functional harmony of the contemporary interior. And since built-ins are designed for many practical purposes, their adaptability often offers exactly the right answers to problems which cannot be solved with single units of furniture alone.

Built-in effects are frequently obtained with movable furniture installed in sections—such as the sectional seating and pole systems described in other chapters of this book. But while the sectional systems are built to be moved, the true built-in is designed to become part of the permanent room architecture. This may involve construction of shelves, counters and cabinets to occupy entire wall areas, or it may be modified to make modular units of furniture fit permanently in certain areas.

As exemplified by the wall furniture for a child's room pictured above, and by the other projects which follow, built-in construction calls for the skill of a carpenter rather than a cabinetmaker.

BUILT-IN CONSTRUCTION

Successful built-in construction depends primarily on accurate cutting of parts. If you have access to a power saw, this is easily performed—or, your lumber dealer may cut the parts for you of a good grade of Western pine, as shown at right.

Framework of built-in furniture is easily assembled prior to hanging on wall. Clear Ponderosa Pine was used here, but less expensive grades of lumber could be used when parts are painted. Nails, screws and glue assure strong assembly of parts.

For this attractive, built-in installation, doors and other parts were pre-painted in contrasting colors. Back boards were secured with screws to wall studding. See plans and descriptive details of following pages.

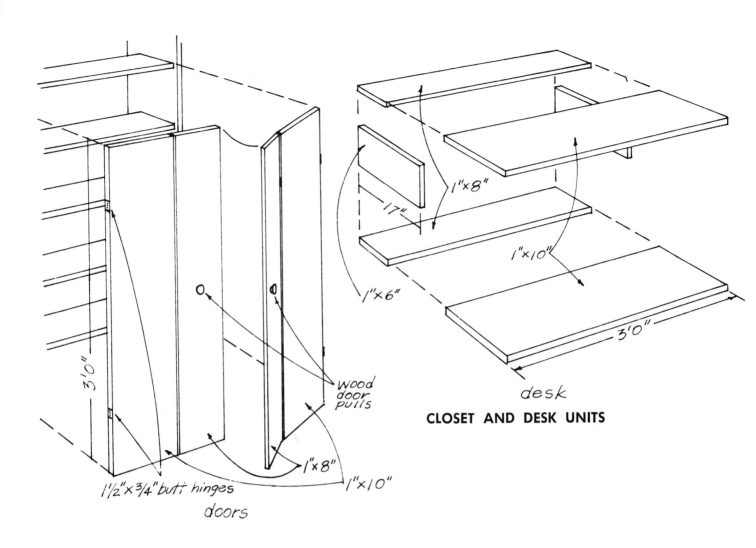

3'0"

1"x8"

17"

1"x6"

1"x8"

1"x10"

wood
door
pulls

1½"x¾" butt hinges

doors

1"x8"

1"x10"

3'0"

1"x10"

desk

CLOSET AND DESK UNITS

BUILT-IN CONSTRUCTION:
CLOSET-SHELF-DESK-BIN UNITS

Compact, built-in units for a child's room, as pictured on page 124, furnish tidy organization of the innumerable odds-ends and requirements of childhood living. There's a place for everything—and everything can be kept in its place to relieve housekeeping chores. Closets with folding doors house hobby equipment and athletic accessories which would otherwise clutter the room. And since everything is mounted on the wall, *no* difficulty will be encountered cleaning the floors underneath.

As detailed on the plan above—and on the facing page—the pre-cut parts are put together in apple pie order. You simply butt and nail the pieces together in the assembly sequence shown on working drawings, and since all components are made of stock lumber, you can do the job at relatively small cost. You may wish to paint the door panels and other parts in contrasting colors. Otherwise, if you prefer to preserve the natural wood graining, stain all parts per instructions of Chapter 9.

SHELVING CONSTRUCTION:
DESK AND BIN UNITS

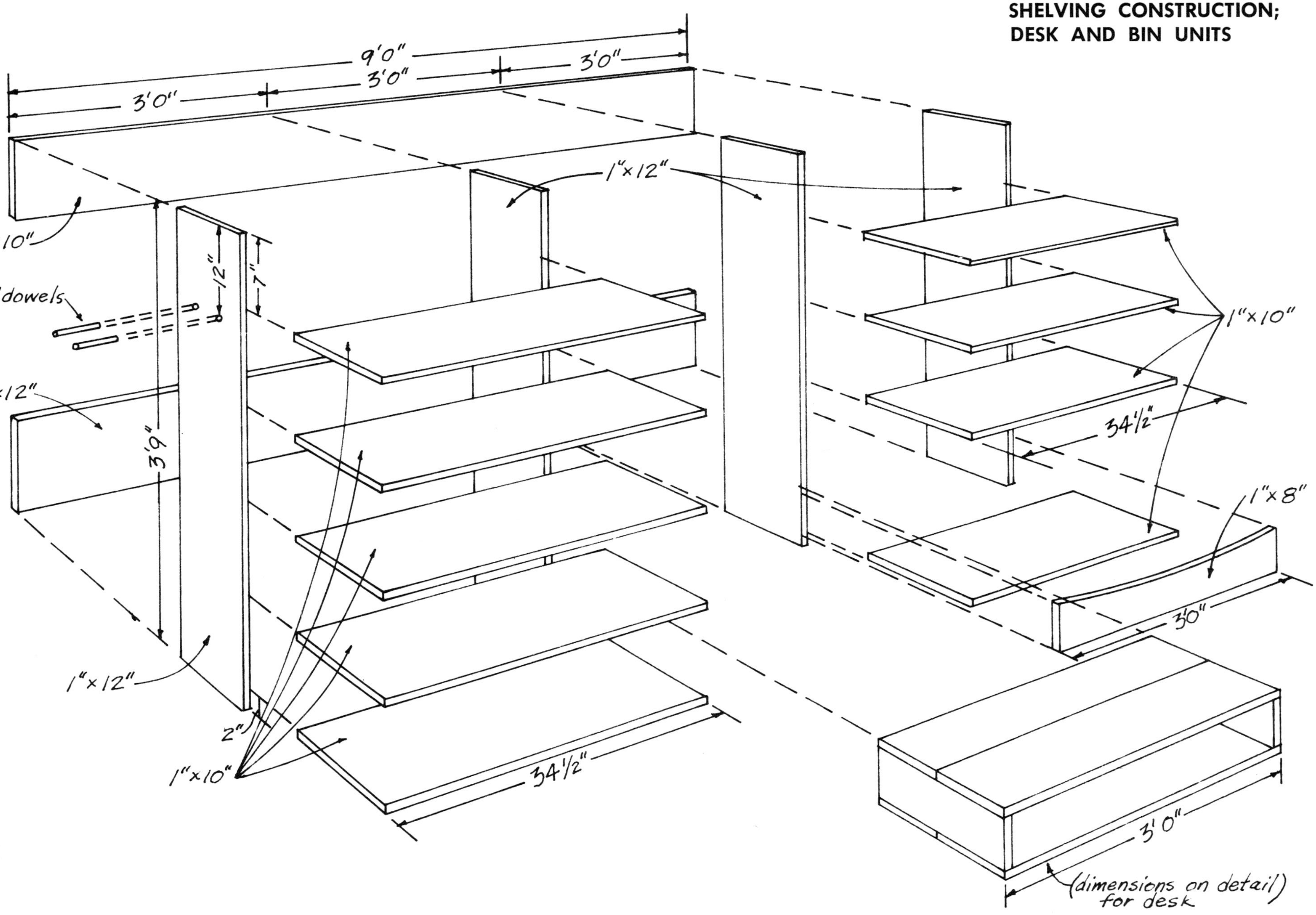

1"x10"

1"x8"

3'0"

3'0"

(dimensions on detail)
for desk

34½"

34½"

1"x12"

1"x10"

2"

9'0"

3'0"

3'0"

3'0"

1"x10"

3/4" dowels

1"x12"

1"x12"

7"

12"R

3'9"

127

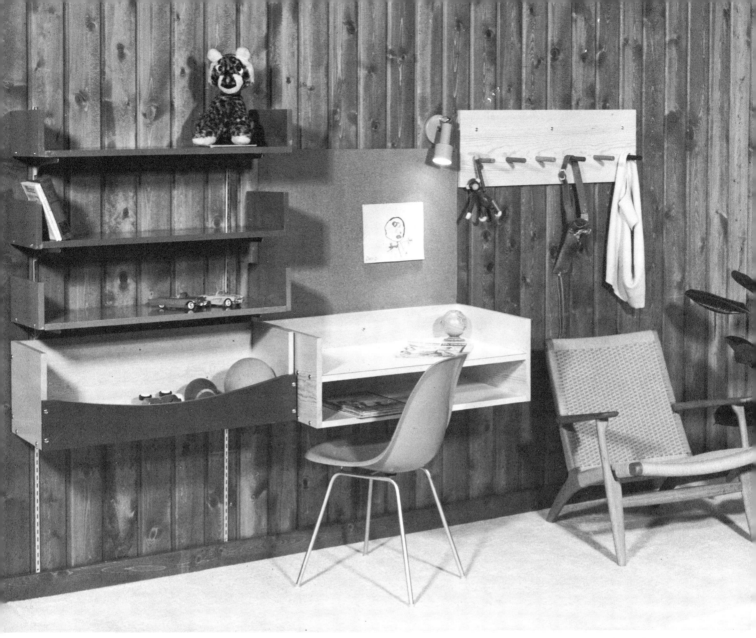

Designs by Don Blair; courtesy Western Wood Products Association

BUILT-IN—
FOR GROWING CHILDREN

A simpler version of built-in furniture for the child's room is illustrated above. This only involves construction of a few shelves, bins, desk box, and pegged board which hangs to the wall. But the interesting feature of this is that the furniture is adjustably mounted to the wall. It can start down low to accommodate toddlers and can then be elevated to keep pace with the growth of the child. This is accomplished with graduated, metal wall standards and brackets on which the end units are adjusted to required heights. The desk and pegged boards are held with a few screws which reach into the studding and are easily redriven for new adjustments.

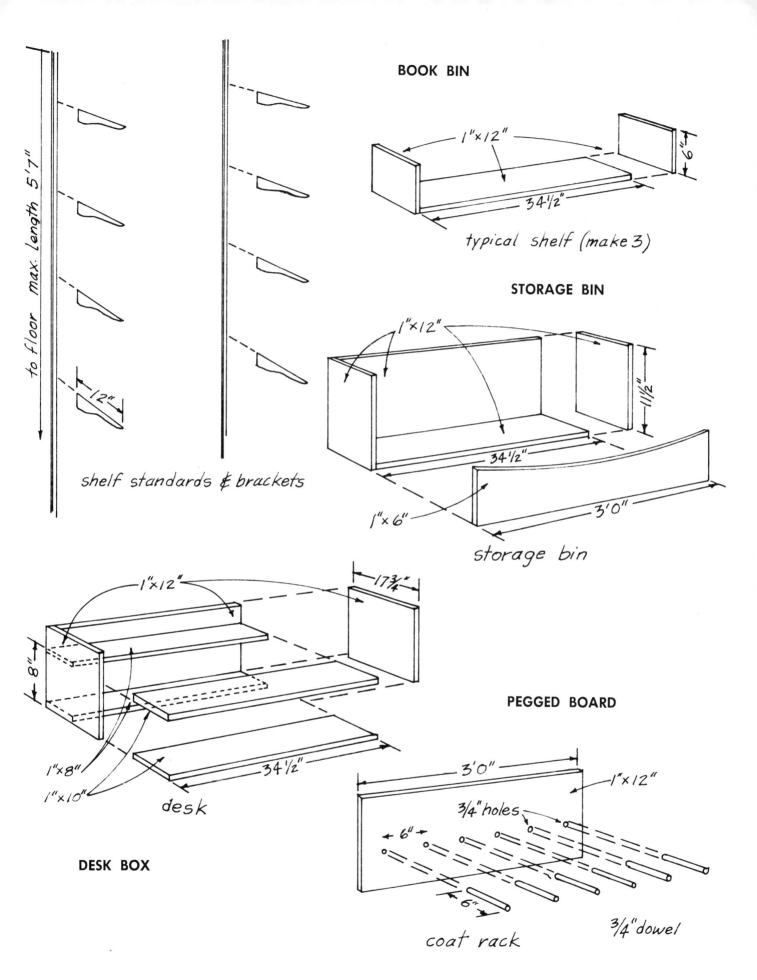

BOOK BIN

1"×12"

6"

34½"

typical shelf (make 3)

STORAGE BIN

1"×12"

11½"

34½"

3'0"

1"×6"

storage bin

to floor max. length 5'7"

12"

shelf standards & brackets

1"×12"

17¾"

8"

1"×8"

1"×10"

34½"

desk

DESK BOX

PEGGED BOARD

3'0"

1"×12"

¾" holes

6"

6"

coat rack

¾" dowel

Courtesy American Plywood Association

BUNK BEDS

This design has been made both functional and attractive by use of pattern cutouts in head and foot uprights, which serve as ladders. Since most children love to climb, getting them to bed will be less of a chore. Beds may be put up or taken down quickly by use of a simple bolted connection at rails and uprights. They can be attached to the wall for additional stability—in case those youngsters of yours are particularly energetic.

CUTTING DIAGRAMS

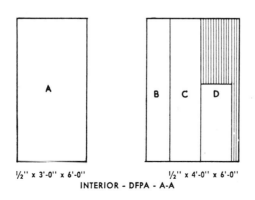

A

½'' x 3'-0'' x 6'-0''
INTERIOR - DFPA - A-A

B C D

½'' x 4'-0'' x 6'-0''

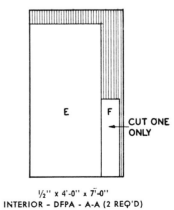

E F

CUT ONE
ONLY

½'' x 4'-0'' x 7'-0''
INTERIOR - DFPA - A-A (2 REQ'D)

130

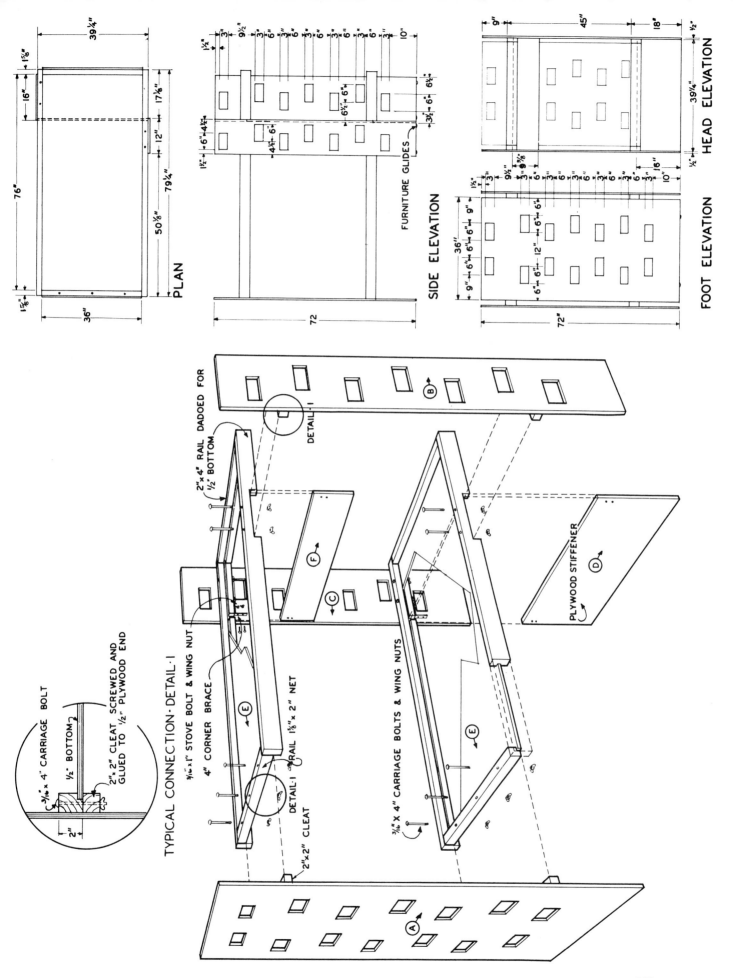

PLAN

SIDE ELEVATION

HEAD ELEVATION

FOOT ELEVATION

FURNITURE GLIDES

DETAIL·1

2" × 4" RAIL DADOED FOR
½" BOTTOM

PLYWOOD STIFFENER

⁹⁄₁₆"×1" STOVE BOLT & WING NUT

4" CORNER BRACE

DETAIL·1 RAIL 1⅝" × 2" NET

2"×2" CLEAT

³⁄₁₆" X 4" CARRIAGE BOLTS & WING NUTS

TYPICAL CONNECTION·DETAIL·1

³⁄₁₆" × 4" CARRIAGE BOLT

½" BOTTOM

2"×2" CLEAT SCREWED AND
GLUED TO ½" PLYWOOD END

2"

131

Labels in the side view detail:
- Beadex
- Redwood cleat holds glass
- Redwood Plywood upright
- 2" x ¾" Redwood Plywood strip to support glass
- notch cleat to fit
- Metal Liner
- 24"
- 12"
- 6"
- 18"
- bottom cleat- each end
- SECTION
- SIDE VIEW DETAIL

Courtesy American Saint Gobain Corporation

PLANTER—DIVIDER

A simpler version of room divider—effective for creating a dramatic entranceway between outside door and living room—is made with a glass-paneled planter. The delicately patterned "Beadex" structural glass also offers a bright solution for the decorative division of areas within a room without sacrificing natural or artificial illumination. By adding a 4″ ceiling board across the top, concealed fluorescent lighting can be installed to illuminate the planting.

Installation of the planter-divider may, at first, give the impression of being a rather formidable undertaking. But an analysis of its construction details indicate there are few complications involved. The uprights and frame pieces are cut from panels of ¾″ plywood to the 24″ widths of plan. Lengths of uprights are determined by the ceiling height. Lengths of the cross members—planter box and ceiling plate—are adjustable to the desired overall width of the built-in structure. You can make it narrow or wide, depending on the amount of room space you want it to occupy. The planter box is simply butted together and fastened with screws. Before inserting the glass panel, stud-fasten the assembly of frame and planter box to wall and ceiling. Structural glass is held between two tapered cleats at each end. Use *exterior-type* plywood for the planter box and line it with metal or plastic bins for your planting. The "Beadex" glass panel can be cut to required size by your glass dealer.

BUILT-IN
FOR DECORATIVE DISPLAY

Sometimes a single narrow window and radiator, intruding upon the decorative treatment of a wall, can be converted from liability to asset simply by building shelves and cabinets around it. The conversion was accomplished here by using Saint Gobain "Huewhite" structural glass for the center shelving. Thus the light shines through to illuminate the decorative objects on the center shelves. In this way, the built-in does double-duty by establishing a focal feature within the contemporary room and furnishing additional shelf and cabinet space. The same idea can be applied to windowless walls by using a mirror behind the center shelves and illuminating, from above, with concealed fluorescent tubes.

As the plan indicates, construction is relatively simple. The 4 uprights are made of 1″ x 10″ lumber, sawed in lengths reaching from floor to ceiling. These are notched in 1½″ at the bottom for the 4″ toe plate. If shelves are to be set in permanently, the top one should be cross-lapped to span the center uprights. Dadoes, ⅜″ deep, should be cut in the uprights to receive shelves. Side shelves are made of ¾″ material; either lumber or plywood. Panel doors are of plywood and the radiator facing panel is made of a sheet of Reynolds DIY aluminum, vented to convey heat, as shown on plan. The Huewhite glass shelves can be cut to required sizes by your glass dealer.

Since this installation is truly built-in, the spread of the center section depends on the width of your window and radiator. The center uprights are fastened to the sides of the window casing. But the outside uprights are screwed to wall cleats fastened to the wall studding. All shelves, including the glass ones of the middle section, can be mounted on Knape & Vogt adjustable shelf strips (obtainable at hardware stores) and set to any desired spacing.

Courtesy American Saint Gobain Corporation

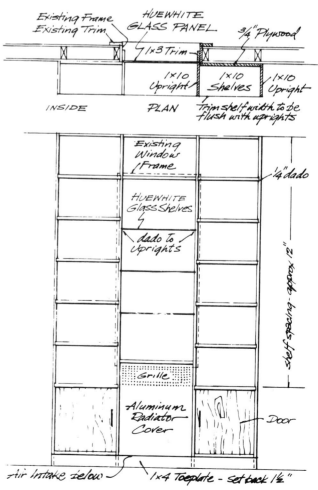

Courtesy Western Wood Products Association

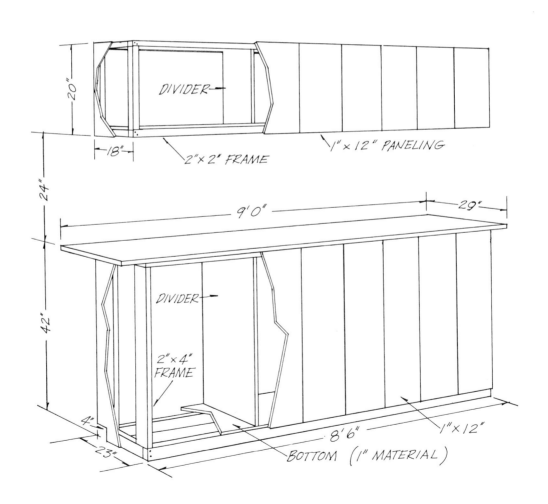

20"

18"

DIVIDER

2" x 2" FRAME

1" x 12" PANELING

24"

9'0"

29"

42"

DIVIDER

2" x 4"
FRAME

4"

23"

8'6"

1" x 12"

BOTTOM (1" MATERIAL)

For a family of growing youngsters, or for any family which entertains and enjoys coffee and snacks at odd hours, there's nothing more convenient than the built-in bars pictured on these pages. They can be installed as dividers between kitchen and dining area, or in a game room where facilities for serving refreshments are required.

Build these bars and cupboards of knotty pine or knotty incense cedar to obtain the natural effects shown in photographs. As the plans indicate, the building of these bars involves only competent carpentry skills. The materials are inexpensive and may be purchased at your local lumber yard. If you are hesitant about attempting the ceramic tile top, shown on the bar at the left, use plywood laminated with Formica, Micarta, or Consoweld. Finally, if you like these ideas, but feel their installation is a bit beyond your carpentry skill, why not call in a carpenter and have him build them for you.

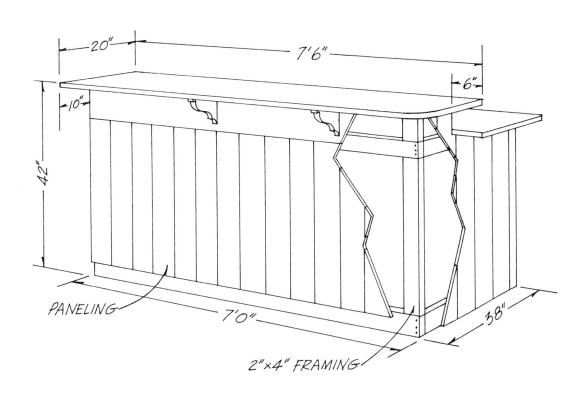

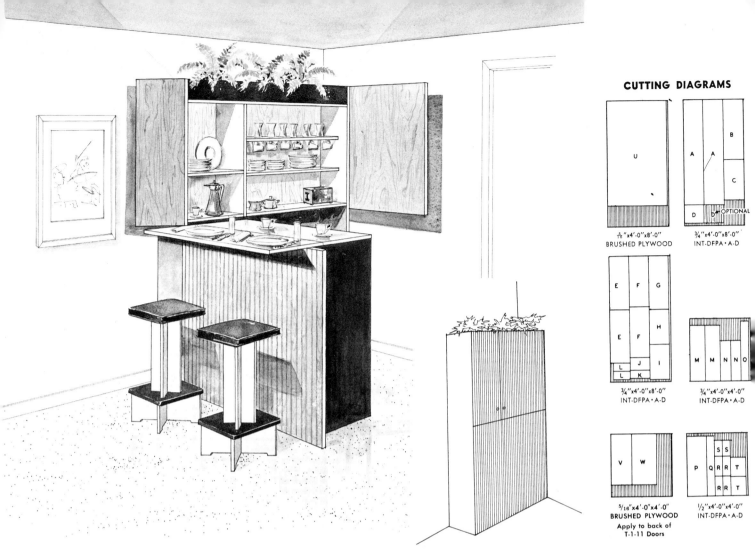

U

⅞″x4′-0″x8′-0″
BRUSHED PLYWOOD

A A B C D D OPTIONAL

¾″x4′-0″x8′-0″
INT·DFPA·A-D

E F G E F H L J I L K

¾″x4′-0″x8′-0″
INT·DFPA·A-D

M M N N O

¾″x4′-0″x4′-0″
INT·DFPA·A-D

V W

⁵⁄₁₆″x4′-0″x4′-0″
BRUSHED PLYWOOD
Apply to back of
T-1-11 Doors

P Q R R T S S R R T

½″x4′-0″x4′-0″
INT·DFPA·A-D

FOLDING BREAKFAST BAR

If your space is limited, you can build a fold-away bar which occupies only a few feet of floor space when folded to closed position. But when the bar is extended and the cabinet doors opened, you will have ample facilities for service, as well as plenty of shelf and closet space for storage of dishes and electrical appliances. This neat arrangement is accomplished with sturdy hinges and base casters on which the bar counter swings out from its wall casing. The top cabinet doors are also strongly hinged to swing open and out of the way when the bar is in use.

Make the folding bar of ¾″ plywood with brushed fir surfaces on the inside and scored paneled effects for the front facing. By following the cutting diagrams above, and the detailed working drawing at the right, the entire unit can be built with ordinary carpentry skills. In fact, you could have it built, to this plan, by a carpenter at relatively small cost. The accompanying bar stools are shown in step-by-step construction on pages 48 to 53. *Bar Design Courtesy American Plywood Association*

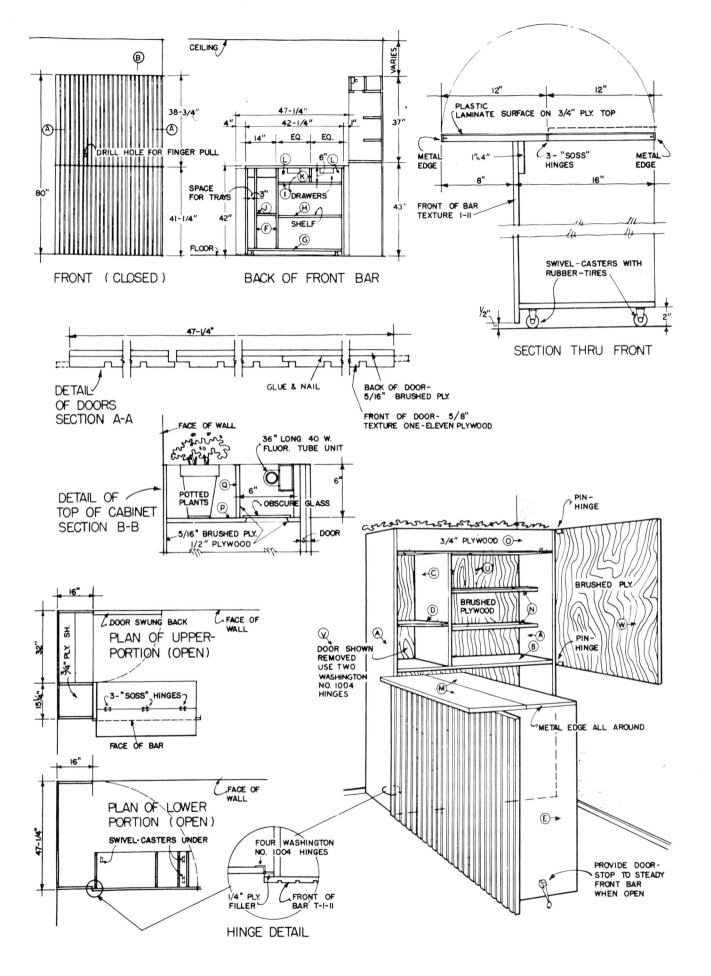

FRONT (CLOSED)

BACK OF FRONT BAR

SECTION THRU FRONT

DETAIL OF DOORS SECTION A-A

GLUE & NAIL

BACK OF DOOR- 5/16" BRUSHED PLY.

FRONT OF DOOR- 5/8" TEXTURE ONE-ELEVEN PLYWOOD

DETAIL OF TOP OF CABINET SECTION B-B

PLAN OF UPPER- PORTION (OPEN)

PLAN OF LOWER PORTION (OPEN)

HINGE DETAIL

HANGING DISH CABINET

When you install this hanging cabinet, you literally make extra storage space where none existed before. In addition to its handsome, modern appearance and simple construction, the sliding doors on both sides make it doubly convenient. You can make the door panels of ¼″ plywood, or you may prefer to use structural glass. By omitting the sliding door panels on one side, you can convert this into a wall cabinet. For this conversion it will only be necessary to attach a plywood panel across the back. Construction is simplified by tracking the panel doors on Reynolds aluminum sliding door tracks which may be purchased at hardware stores. *Courtesy American Plywood Association*

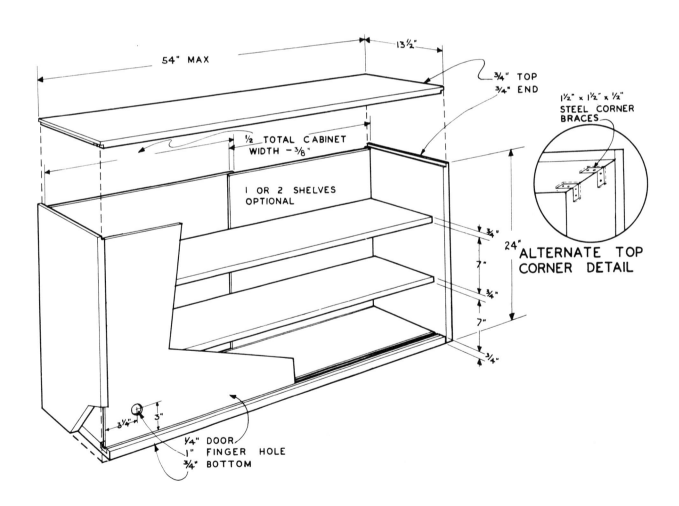

OVERHEAD FLUORESCENT STORAGE

By the time you've squeezed a modern washer, dryer and a hamperful of dirty clothes into a kitchen laundry area, there's little space left for storage. Why not mount a cabinet for soaps and supplies on the wall above one of the counters? The one shown, a box with shelves built from ¾″ plywood, features a fluorescent light behind the top facing to illuminate whatever is on the shelves. As the plan indicates, there's nothing complicated about this built-in cabinet. Its construction requires nothing more than nailing together the parts of given dimensions. *Courtesy American Plywood Association*

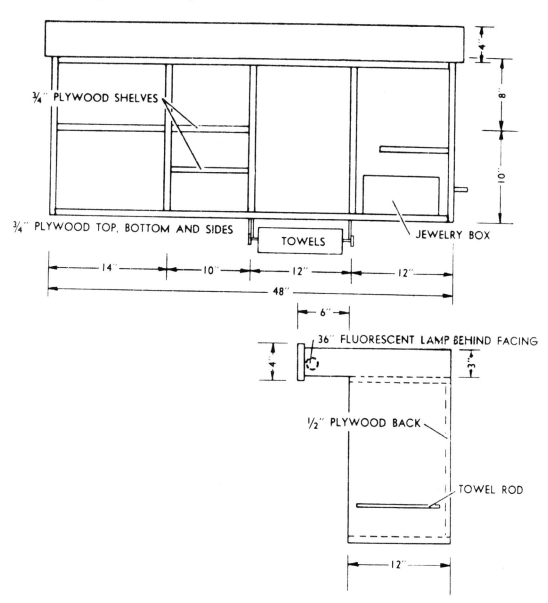

¾″ PLYWOOD SHELVES

¾″ PLYWOOD TOP, BOTTOM AND SIDES

TOWELS

JEWELRY BOX

8″

10″

14″   10″   12″   12″

48″

6″

36″ FLUORESCENT LAMP BEHIND FACING

4″

3″

½″ PLYWOOD BACK

TOWEL ROD

12″

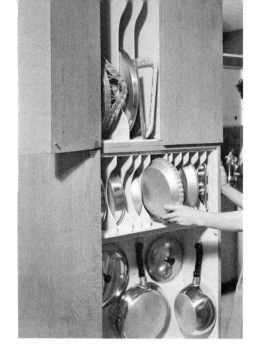

UTENSIL CABINET

There's always the problem of finding a place to put pots, pans, trays, and bulky oven utensils. So why not build this handy cabinet which was designed just for this purpose? Provision is even made in the plan for installation of a wall oven. But if your stove has its own oven, use this space for additional storage. *Courtesy American Plywood Association*

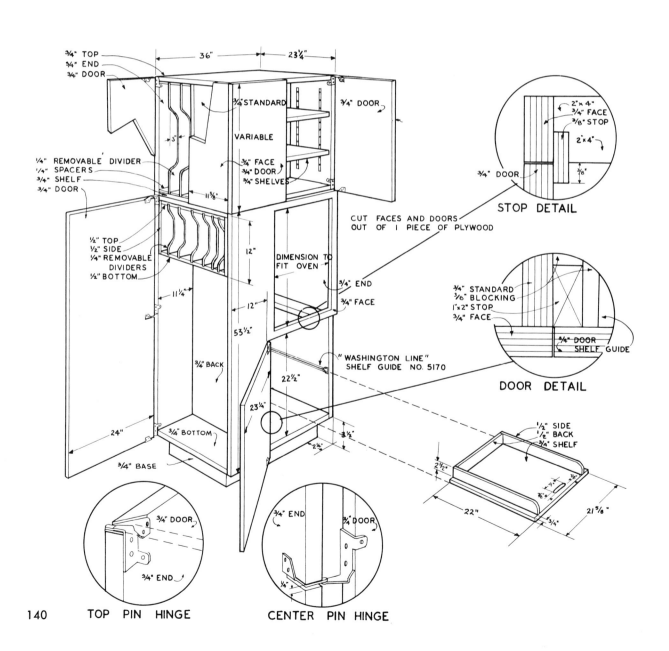

7

CONTEMPORARY COMPONENTS & KITS

All sectional components designed by Poul Cadovius; courtesy Royal System

SECTIONAL FURNITURE

You will observe that sectional furniture goes well in practically every room of the house and, as demonstrated here, it blends with traditional as well as contemporary decor. Among the many interchangeable units—desks, cabinets, cases, shelves, drawer components, racks and tables—you can pick attractive pieces for furnishing living room, bedroom, dining room, study, playroom, and other areas. And you will welcome the additional storage space and efficient organization which these units provide.

The "Royal System" arrangements, shown here and on following pages, are among the most illustrative of the various decorative effects which can be had with this fine furniture. As described and demonstrated on the following six pages, they are superbly crafted and engineered for easy installation. These units are made of walnut and teak with hand-rubbed, natural oil finishes, as described in Chapter 9.

Because it has become one of the most significant developments of contemporary design, much space in this book is devoted to numerous applications of sectional furniture. As illustrated here, and elsewhere throughout this book, sectional furniture offers entirely new concepts of functional room furnishing. It is adaptable to any type, size, or shape of room and it is flexible to be expanded or contracted with interchangeable modular units forming myriads of different arrangements.

But the fundamental appeal of the sectional idea is its ideal adaptability to your "freedom of choice" for planning individual rooms. With sectional pieces, you become your own decorator and designer.

From the innumerable furniture components illustrated here and on following pages, you can choose exactly what you want and need, and you can assemble your selection on wall standards or mid-area tension poles to suit your own decorative scheme. Moreover, you can start modestly, with a few units, and later amplify your basic arrangement with additional "open stock" components.

A "working wall" is furnished with table, chests and shelves to produce this attractive arrangement.

Sectional furniture blends with any type of decor. These units are wall-hung in the dining area to produce this functional effect.

You can turn corners with decorative wall sectionals as illustrated in this bedroom.

The contemporary interior, divided with pole-hung sectional components, offers a bonus of storage space as well as contributing to tasteful decor. This pole divider is flanked on both sides with spacious chests and shelves to absorb the overflow of books, magazines and objets d'art which accumulate about the living room. The next six pages explain installation and show a variety of optional arrangements.

Sectional components courtesy Royal System

SECTIONAL COMPONENTS

Here are the sectional furniture components. They range from simple shelves to neatly compartmented desks, chests and cabinets. But they have one thing in common: they are all engineered to hang securely between poles and wall standards. This is accomplished with simple, metal clasps on the back of each case unit. These lock to steel pins inserted through holes in the wall standards and poles. Since these holes are bored at 1½″ intervals along the length of poles and standards, the sectional units can be mounted at variable heights and spacing. The mounting of shelves is even simpler. They rest on steel nibs and are suspended by wire fixtures which insert into the pre-drilled holes. The assembly is detailed in photographs on the facing page.

Shelves, depths: 7⅞″, 9½″, 11¾″, 14¾″, 15¾″.
Television shelf, 19″ deep

Television shelf, 15¾″ deep

Corner television shelf, 14¾″ deep

3 drawer chest, 16¾″ high, 14¾″ deep

Bar-cabinet. Drop-lid (resists liquor) with front of woven veneer, rack for 8 bottles, 2 trays, 16¾″ high, 14¾″ deep

Storage cabinet. Drop-li with front of woven ve neer, adjustable shelf, 16¾″ high, 14¾″ dee

Record cabinet. Drop-lid with front of woven veneer, removable record dividers. 16¾″ high, 14¾″ deep

Desk. Drop-lid with front of woven veneer, 4 small trays, partitions. 16¾″ high, 14¾″ deep

Loud-speaker unit. ¾ plywood front and bac Baffle cloth included. I side m. 9½″x13⅜″x30 15″ high, 11¾″ deep.

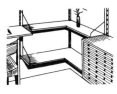

Corner shelves, depths: 7⅞″, 9½″, 11¾″.

Magazine shelves, depths: 11¾″, 13¾″.

Desk with 2 draw 3½″ high, 14¾″ de 3½″ high, 15¾″ de

Storage cabinet. Plain-front sliding doors, adjustable shelf, 16¾″ high, 14¾″ deep

4 drawer chest, 20¼″ high, 15¾″ deep

Drop-lid with front of v ven veneer, 2 draw above, adjustable shelf 20¼″ high, 15¾″ de

144

K-table,
  depth 47¼'', width 31½'', height 28'',
  each flap 23⅝'',
  length with flaps up 94½''

R-table,
  depth 41¼'', flap 21½'', height 29'',
  width 31½''

Cabinet with glass sliding
doors and adjustable shelf
13¼'' high, 9½'' deep

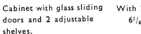

Cabinet with glass sliding
doors and 2 adjustable
shelves,
  22'' high, 9½'' deep

With 2 drawers,
  6¼'' high, 11¾'' deep

With 2 drawers, 2 spaces
above,
  9½'' high, 11¾'' deep

With desk, plain front,
  13¼'' high, 11¾'' deep

Drawer on steel slides for
changer for unit 21,
  4½'' high, 12¼'' deep

For tuner, amplifier, tape-
recorder and changer. 2
loose shelves, 1 front panel.
Inside m. 13⅜'' x 18¾'' x
30''.
  20¼'' high, 15¾'' deep

With plain-front sliding
doors, center partition, 2
shelves on both sides,
  20¼'' high, 15¾'' deep

Pia chair,
  29'' high, 18¾'' wide,
in teak or walnut-col-
ored beech. Craft-cord
seat.

Lamp. Attached to a rail.

Book end. Black metal

Components of spring-loaded pole include padded
top disk to protect ceiling.

Bottom of pole is adjusted with steel pin to secure
proper tension at ceiling height.

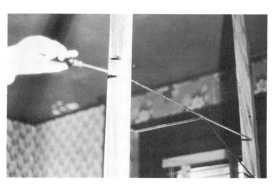

Wire spacers fit between poles to assure accuracy
of space and alignment.

Back of shelf rests on steel nibs. Shelf is suspended
on wire fixtures. Cabinet hangs on two steel pins.

Sectional components courtesy Royal System

Here are the sectional furniture units for assembly of the divider installation, shown above.

HOW TO INSTALL A SECTIONAL ROOM DIVIDER

Installation of tension poles to hang sectional furniture units, such as those illustrated above, requires only the patience of putting up poles at proper spacing and in true alignment. Poles should be purchased in lengths measuring approximately 6″ less than ceiling height. As shown on the previous page, they are then adjusted at the bottom so that the spring-loaded top maintains just enough pressure on the ceiling for a firm fit. (If they are too tight, excessive pressure on the ceiling may damage the plaster.) Since your first chore will be to locate the pole positions *on the ceiling*, where their placement starts, make light pencil marks on the ceiling, at right angles to the wall, to indicate where the pole tops are centered at 32″ intervals. If you are unsure about alignment, a large square of cardboard, held flush against the wall, will guide the right-angle marking.

The spring-loaded top of the pole is then centered and pressed over the ceiling mark and by putting pressure on the top, the bottom of the pole can be moved in along the floor for perpendicular alignment. This must be checked and adjusted with a spirit level to be sure it is perfectly perpendicular. Following the same procedure, successive poles, for the Royal installation, are then fitted exactly 30½″ apart. The exact spread can be secured with the spacer brackets which fit between the poles.

Sectional units, such as those illustrated, are notched at the top to fit snugly within the precise 30½″ spacing of poles. They hang between the poles on metal top clasps which are secured with steel pins inserted through the poles.

146

1 Measure out at right angle to wall and make pencil dots on ceiling, at 32" intervals, to mark center locations of pole tops.

2 Press spring-loaded top of pole over center mark on ceiling and move floor end into perpendicular position.

3 Check perpendicular alignment of pole with spirit level. Perfect alignment and spacing must be secured.

4 Spacing between poles is checked with measuring board and is then secured with spacer brackets.

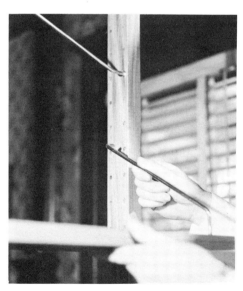

5 Shelves rest on metal nibs inserted in poles and are suspended with wire brackets which fit into holes.

6 Cabinet units notch snugly between poles and are supported with steel pins.

Courtesy of Royal System

HOW TO INSTALL
SECTIONAL WALL UNITS

Sectional wall furniture is relatively easy to install, *BUT*—the "but" is a big one because this furniture must be securely hung to avoid any possibility of its tearing loose from the wall during subsequent use. To avoid this possibility, be sure to attach the standards to solid studding —or, use anchor bolts or "mollys" which hold firmly behind the plaster lath. The wooden wall standards are pre-drilled at 1½" intervals to receive the pins and brackets which support sectional components. They are fastened to the walls on 32" centers of stud spacing which allows parallel space of 30½" between standards.

The step-by-step procedures pictured here should be followed for attaching any type of standards to wall studding. As a rule all types of supporting strips are attached on 32" centers.

1 Studding is located by tapping wall for *solid sound* which differs from sound of hollow plaster.

4 Top end of standard is screwed to wall over stud location.

7 Steel pins, for securing cabinets, are inserted through holes of standards.

2 Needle-point drill is used to test wall at presumed location of stud. Test is made above and below.

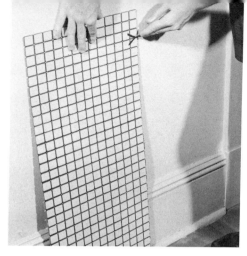

3 Desired location of bottom end of standard is lightly marked on wall.

5 Standard is adjusted with spirit level for perpendicular alignment.

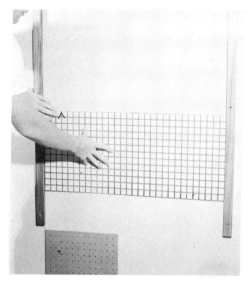

6 Parallel spacing between standards is checked before final fastening of next strip.

8 Cabinet hangs on steel pins. This desk unit was adjusted with counter 28" high.

9 Sectional furniture, assembled on wall standards, produces functional and decorative effects.

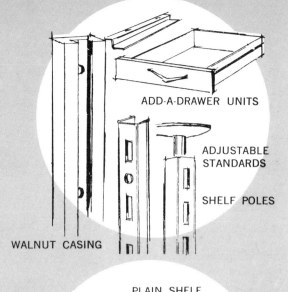

ADD-A-DRAWER UNITS

ADJUSTABLE STANDARDS

SHELF POLES

WALNUT CASING

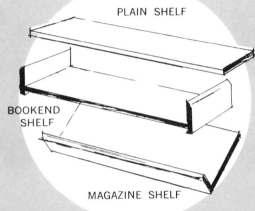

PLAIN SHELF

BOOKEND SHELF

MAGAZINE SHELF

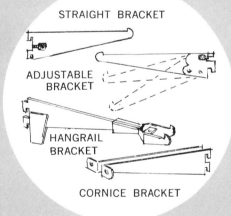

STRAIGHT BRACKET

ADJUSTABLE BRACKET

HANGRAIL BRACKET

CORNICE BRACKET

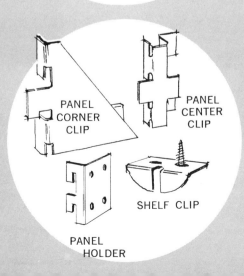

PANEL CORNER CLIP

PANEL CENTER CLIP

SHELF CLIP

PANEL HOLDER

SKETCHBOOK OF SECTIONAL SHELVING AND STORAGE IDEAS

As sketched here and on the following four pages, there appears to be no limit to the arrangements possible with contemporary pole systems and wall-hung units. Furthermore these are easy, do-it-yourself, ideas, accomplished with the standard hardware and fittings sketched at the left.

With sectional installations you can add new dimensions to your home; expand the functional and decorative possibilities of your walls, corners, and central areas to suit your own tastes and needs. You can design your own adjustable storage systems to blend with your interior decor. Special accessories—stereo, hi-fi, television, and hobby collections—can have their own custom-designed housing of shelves and cabinets, located and arranged to suit your individual requirements.

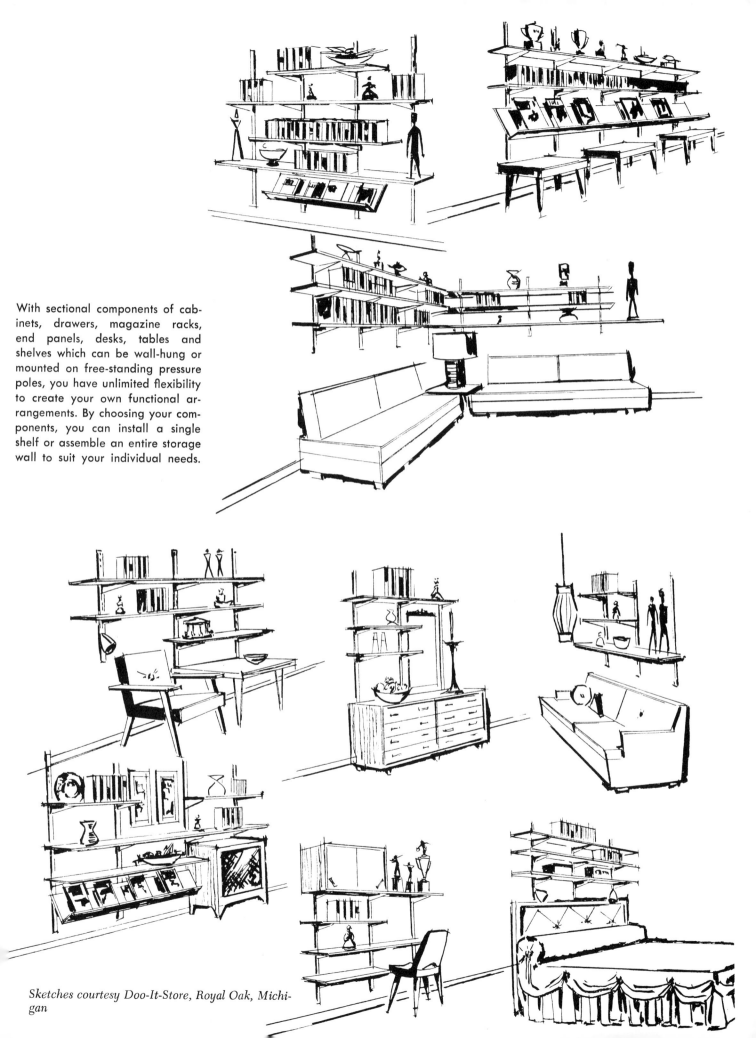

With sectional components of cabinets, drawers, magazine racks, end panels, desks, tables and shelves which can be wall-hung or mounted on free-standing pressure poles, you have unlimited flexibility to create your own functional arrangements. By choosing your components, you can install a single shelf or assemble an entire storage wall to suit your individual needs.

Sketches courtesy Doo-It-Store, Royal Oak, Michigan

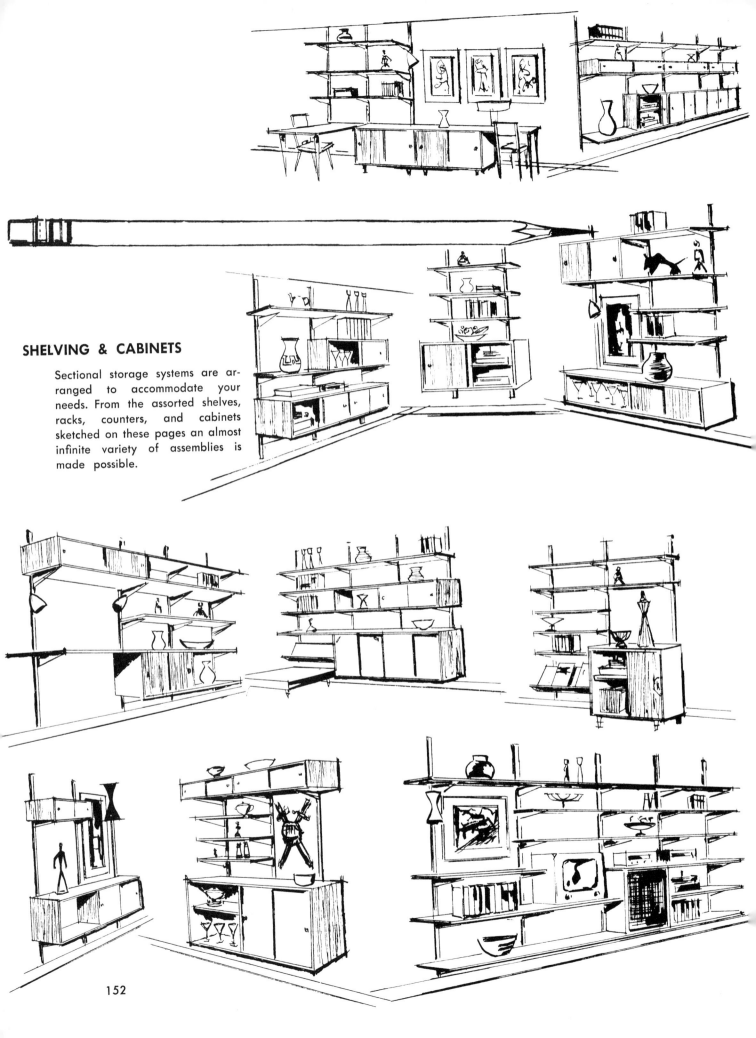

SHELVING & CABINETS

Sectional storage systems are arranged to accommodate your needs. From the assorted shelves, racks, counters, and cabinets sketched on these pages an almost infinite variety of assemblies is made possible.

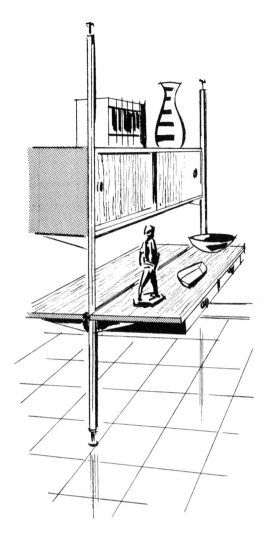

SPACE DIVIDERS

With pressure-poles which stand free of walls to support a variety of sectional units, you can create your own designs for inner space. These spring-loaded poles are softly padded to prevent damage to floor or ceiling. Dozens of dramatic room divider ideas can be constructed with them. As sketched on this page, you can make attractive dividers to go between living room and dining areas—a floor to ceiling library, or a floating island of cabinets and shelves.

Sketches courtesy Doo-It-Store, Royal Oak, Michigan

FOR CHILDREN'S ROOMS

Here are some sectional wall ideas for a child's room which keep pace with your youngster's growth. You can mount these units low to accommodate toddlers and then, as they grow, you can elevate them, inch by inch on the adjustable wall standards. The special brackets are easily changed to the proper slots and clips are available to hold blackboard, pegboard, or mirror.

PEGBOARD

BLACKBOARD

MIRROR

FUNCTIONAL PARTITIONING

Attractive partitions are easily installed with pressure poles. They are used to divide play rooms, children's bedrooms or general living areas. Center panels are made of plywood, Masonite, pegboard or canvas. Combined with shelving or cabinets, these partitions do double-duty by creating privacy on both sides.

Sketches courtesy Doo-It-Store, Royal Oak, Michigan

It will be observed there are many different types and makes of sectional wall systems. The imported versions, shown at the right, use wooden wall standards and overlapping wire fixtures for the shelves.

Courtesy Door Store, Washington, D.C.

Another type of sectional furniture is suspended on standards which are screw-adjusted to floor and ceiling. As pictured below, and to the right, these adjustable standards are used singly against the wall, or locked together to form two sides of a room divider.

Courtesy Brown-Saltman Corporation

If you are artistically inclined, you will certainly enjoy creating your own decorative designs of sectional furniture. The attractive Mondrian-like composition, pictured at the left, shows what can be done. By using these modular components as creative materials, you can give free expression to your imagination in the construction of your own individualized designs.

Courtesy Door Store, Washington, D.C.

155

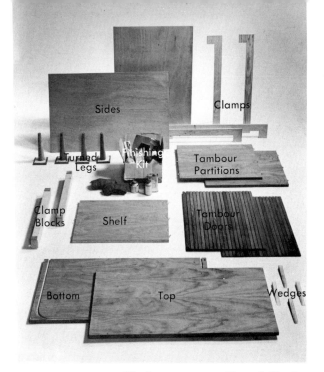

All photos courtesy Furn-A-Kit, Inc.

All parts of the attractive cabinet pictured, at the left, are pre-processed for easy assembly. Hardware, adhesives, and finishing materials are included. You even get clamps to hold the glued parts together.

HOW TO ASSEMBLE CONTEMPORARY FURNITURE WITH KITS OF PRE-CUT PARTS

Even if you can't saw a board in half—or, lack the tools to do so—you can still produce handsome contemporary furniture, on the do-it-yourself plan, with the furniture kits shown on these pages. Furthermore, you can assemble and finish this furniture yourself at a fraction of the cost of fully manufactured pieces of equivalent value.

As pictured here, furniture kits come in knock-down form with all parts fully processed for easy assembly. Clear, step-by-step instructions and diagrams are given to guide construction. This requires little more in the way of tools than a hammer and screwdriver. All incidentals needed to guarantee successful results are included. You get all the hardware, adhesives and finishing materials—even wooden clamps with which to assemble the parts.

1 Assembly starts by gluing together the predoweled case panels.

2 Wooden clamps, furnished with kit, secure the glued joints during drying period.

3 Tambour doors are inserted in pre-cut grooves. Back is made of single panel.

4 Base parts are glued and screw-fastened. Optional base designs are available.

5 Finished cabinet has professional look of fine custom-built furniture.

All photos courtesy Furn-A-Kit, Inc.

YOUR CHOICE
OF KIT DESIGNS

The contemporary furniture pictured here represents just a few of the many attractive designs which may be constructed with kits. These range from benches to highboys to mirror frames and include knock-down units for easy assembly of modular installations. All of them are superbly styled and can be assembled even by the novice homecrafter to produce professional results. The "fool-proof" secret of these kits is the precision with which all parts are precut and prefitted at the factory. This, together with the detailed instructions and plans which accompany each kit, guides every step of assembly.

158

Even the larger items are easily assembled. Meticulous instructions accompany each kit. Every step is very clearly described down to the most minute detail. And you get all the hardware and incidentals needed to do the complete job at approximately one-half the cost of factory-finished furniture of equivalent design-value.

Pictured at the right is a detail of the slanted-dowel construction which assures exceptionally strong joinery when secured with glue. Clamps and glue come with kits together with instructions on how to assemble all joints.

Carefully crafted furniture deserves a fine, professional-appearing finish and the kit manufacturers provide the best. You have a choice of oil or semi-gloss finish. Since the parts have all been machine sanded at the factory, they only require fine hand-sanding prior to application of finish.

In final treatment any slight surface imperfections caused by glue splotches are carefully removed with sandpaper. Cracks and dents are filled with wood dough matching the wood color. A sanding block is then used for final, overall sanding which should be done in the direction of the grain.

When a natural oil finish is applied to teak or walnut, it is only necessary to let the oil penetrate and then wipe away the excess with a soft cloth. For luster finishes, several coats are applied, rubbing between coats with fine steel wool. All finishing materials come with kits.

All photos courtesy Furn-A-Kit, Inc.

8

HOW TO COVER & UPHOLSTER CONTEMPORARY FURNITURE

HOW TO APPLY SURFACING MATERIALS

You may want to cover the top surface of a table, cabinet or counter with an attractive and durable material which will contribute to the functional fitness of the design and offer an interesting surface contrast to the woods used in construction. This is often desirable when broad plywood panels are used for table tops with bases made of rich-grained solid woods.

As suggested by the above illustration, you will find a wide range of surfacing materials from which to select. These come in plastics, leathers, tiles, vinyls, as well as rich veneers of fine-grained woods. They can be obtained in sheets and rolls of various tones and textures. Of particular interest are the vinyl coverings which come in colors and surface patterns to simulate tooled leather and other effects. These are durable and easy to keep clean.

Application of surfacing materials, as demonstrated in the following step-by-step photo sequences, is relatively easy. They are bonded to the wood surfaces either with their own type of adhesive (as designated with the material) or with contact cement. The beginner should be cautioned, however, that contact cement can be a highly treacherous adhesive, if not properly used. It makes an instant bond which cannot be torn loose for resetting.

Covering a Plywood Top with Armstrong Vinyl

1 Adhesive is brushed on plywood surface.

2 Under surface of Armstrong vinyl covering is brushed with adhesive.

3 Covering is placed over plywood disk and rolled flat.

4 Edges are trimmed with sharp knife.

162

Covering a Counter with Service Corlon

If you need a serviceable counter-top for your side chests or cabinets, here is how to make one. Use the flexible vinyl covering called "Counter Corlon." First take the top measurements of your cabinet allowing proper overlap. Add 4⅛″ to cutting dimensions of the width. This is sawed off to make the 4″ backboard. Shape a ⅜″ quarter-round along one edge of the counter and backboard. Then proceed with construction as shown in the following step-by-step, photo sequence.

Photo-sequence courtesy Armstrong Cork Company.

1 Here's everything the job requires. The ¾-inch strip in the middle is used as a braceboard.

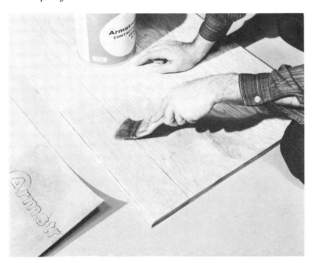

2 Brush adhesive on the plywood surface and on back of the vinyl covering.

3 Apply vinyl covering with overlap along edges. The 4-inch backboard rests flush to edge of counter, ready to be bent perpendicular after adhesive sets.

4 Backboard is bent up at right angle to plywood surface and bracing strip is glued and nailed along back edges.

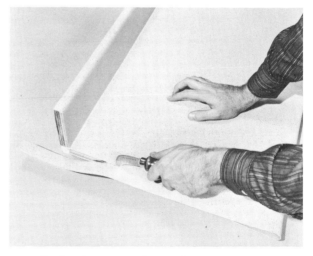

5 Overlapping edges of covering are trimmed with linoleum knife. End edges can be covered with same material.

HOW TO VENEER CONTEMPORARY FURNITURE

The art of veneering dates back many centuries. But the techniques involved have never been so readily available to the layman as they are now with a reinforced veneer product called "Flexwood." Flexwood is made by the U.S. Plywood Corporation in standard sheets measuring 4' x 8'. It comes in a variety of rich woods. Its exquisitely matched graining would be practically impossible to duplicate in any selection of stock lumber. But the beauty of this veneer is that it is *real wood*, prepared in thin sheets that can be handled as easily as wallpaper.

Because of the tendency of solid lumber to expand and contract with seasonal changes of climate, Flexwood cannot be used over it. But it can be applied to any stable surface such as plywood and smooth composition materials.

Depending on the type of adhesives used, it is relatively easy to bond Flexwood to a plywood or composition surface. This is done either with its own paste-like adhesive or with contact cement. The Flexwood adhesive is slower drying and thus allows some tolerance of time for resetting the veneer, in case it wasn't properly adjusted at first try. But with contact cement the veneer goes on *for keeps—the moment the contact is made!* On the instant of touch, the veneer becomes part of the surface— and any accidents of uneven fit, ripples or bulges in the veneer cannot be corrected once the contact bond has been made.

The big advantage of using contact cement is that it provides an absolute and everlasting bond. The veneer becomes part of the surface. For this reason, the correct procedures for using it are detailed in the following, step-by-step photo sequence showing how the "Tumble-Table," (featured on pages 60 to 66) was actually veneered with Flexwood. If you follow these steps, you may avoid "contact calamities." *But do be aware of the hazards involved!*

1 Flexwood comes in sheets measuring 4' x 8'. Note beautifully matched graining of this walnut veneer. Other fine woods are available.

4 Razor-blade knife and steel straight edge are used to cut veneer to exact size.

7 Masking tape holds veneer lightly in place over paper slip-sheet. Paper is slightly withdrawn while starting contact between veneer and surface is made at one end.

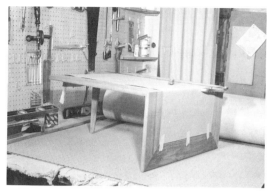

2 Precise paper pattern is made of center area of table to be Flexwood veneered.

3 Lines are squared on veneer, marking exact size of table area to be covered.

5 Contact cement is brushed on back side of veneer. It is then brushed on center panel of table to which veneer will be bonded.

6 After contact cement has been given thirty minutes to become *surface dry* to the touch, the paper is inserted to act as a slip-sheet between impregnated table top and veneer.

8 With one end fully contacted, top flap of veneer is lifted and pressed over corner for firm fit along edge of top surface.

9 Inch by inch, with even pressure of hands, the paper slip-sheet is gradually withdrawn. Smoothing pressure secures lasting contact.

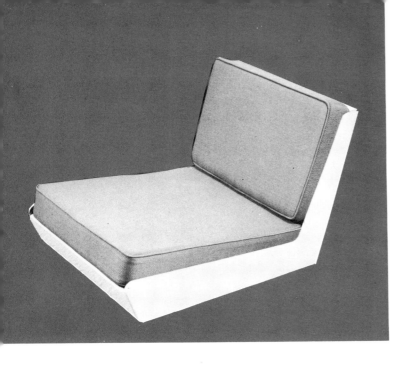

Beveled slots are sawed in frame of seat platform to receive metal clips of "Elastaseat" panel.

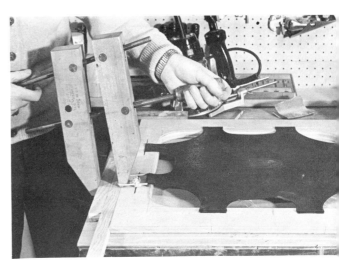

"Elastaseat" is stretched with clamp to insert end clips in beveled slots of seat platform.

UPHOLSTERING— RESILIENT PLATFORM CONSTRUCTION

When you stop to consider the procedures involved in traditional upholstering of furniture, you will agree that the new materials and techniques used to create soft, contemporary seating come as a blessing. For while it was traditionally maintained that you could not produce comfortable upholstery without introducing bulk quantities of springs, burlap, feathers, horsehair, and padding, the contemporary designer eliminates all this and still produces lounge seating of luxurious comfort. To accomplish this he discards the heavy and bulky materials and uses in their place, lightweight and efficient cushioning of urethane or rubber foam on resilient platforms made of elasticized webbing or rubber stretch panels. And the resulting upholstery is not only as comfortable as before, it is also far more durable and easier to maintain. No longer do burlap tacks come loose in the bottom platforms of easy chairs to cause sags and spill padding. With stretch-web platforms, there are no springs to work loose and stab through covering materials. And the hourly chore of "plumping up" feather, down or kapok cushions is eliminated entirely when foam-fillings are used, for foam retains its shape without "plumping."

Assembled seat platform is ready to be attached to seating unit.

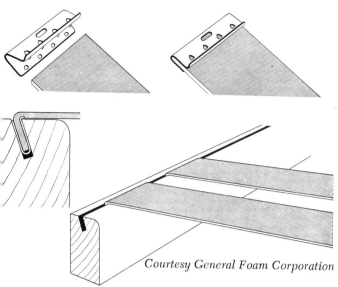

Beveled groove secures metal end clips of "Pirelli" webbing.

Even the effects of "heavy" upholstery are now obtained with platforms of resilient webbing and light-weight foam cushioning and padding.

Press-on, clip webbing, combined with foam cushions, assures seating comfort of contemporary chairs and sofas.

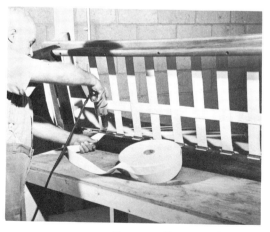

Platform is attached industrially from roll of "Diatex" webbing. Screw-on clamps secure the ends under proper tension.

But one of the chief appeals of the new upholstery is that it provides comfort without excessive weight. You don't have to struggle with heavy and bulky chairs and sofas when it's time to vacuum under and around them.

As an example, the sectional seating-unit illustrated here, while providing a maximum of softness and comfort, actually weighs less than twenty pounds. The resilient seat platform is made with an Acushnet "Elastaseat" stretch-panel, while the cushions are of light-weight du Pont derivative, urethane foam. This seating unit is used to make the luxurious chairs and sofas detailed in Chapter 4. Its construction is demonstrated in step-by-step photographs on pages 54 to 59.

Other types of light-weight resilient seat platforms are made with the "Pirelli" and "Diatex" strap webbing shown on this page. This is manufactured of a tough, rubber composition. It is stretched to form lattice-like platforms of various shapes. Strap webbing is installed either with metal, end-clips which fit into beveled grooves of the frame, as sketched above, or with screw-on clamps as pictured at the bottom right. It can be purchased at houseware or upholstery shops.

HOW TO UPHOLSTER
WITH URETHANE FOAM

Light-weight urethane foam, derived of Du
Pont Hylene and Freon, can be purchased by
the yard, or in slabs of standard dimensions, to
make soft and durable cushions. Urethane foam
has the ability to retain its shape. When used
for cushions and arm rests such as those shown
with the lounge chair, above, and the round
ottoman, at the right, it combines with appropriate fabrics to produce an exceptionally neat
and well-tailored appearance.

As demonstrated in photo-sequences of following pages, which show how the cushions and
arm rests were actually upholstered, these results are not too difficult to obtain. Anyone own-
ing a sewing machine and having the ability to
use it, can follow these steps of foam cushion
construction, or a competent seamstress can
make the covers for you.

Materials used here were 4″ thick urethane
foam measuring 24″ x 28″ for seat cushions 18″
x 24″ for back cushion and 36″ diameter for
ottoman. "Cohama" fabrics, treated with Du
Pont, soil-resistant "Zepel," were used for the
covering.

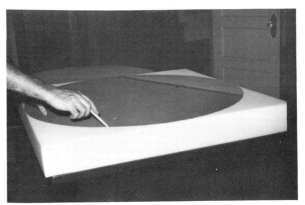

Slab of 4″ urethane is marked with ball-point
pen to circular pattern of ottoman cushions.

Urethane foam is easily cut on bandsaw. Coping
saw or sharp knife, can also be used.

1 Materials for making square cushions include precut urethane foam, welting cord, thread, fabric, yardstick and sharp scissors.

2 Edges and corners of foam are chamfered ¼'' to soften the lines.

3 Face and side panels of cushion are cut only slightly larger than actual foam dimensions, to assure snug, tailored fit.

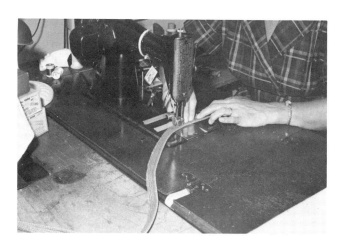

4 Strip of self-welting, bias cut from fabric, is stitched over welting cord.

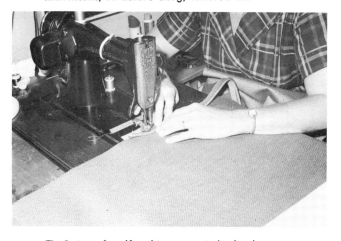

5 Strip of self-welting is stitched along edge, on off side of facing panel. Opposite flap is then stitched to side panel.

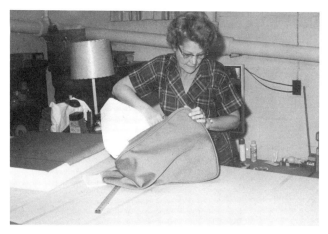

6 Cover is reversed with welt stitching on inside and foam filler is inserted. Final closure, at back, is hand stitched.

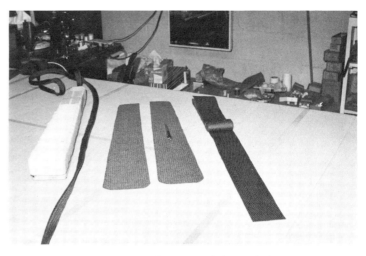

1 For foam upholstered chair arms, cardboard pattern of arm shape is first marked on fabric. Panels are cut slightly oversize to allow for welting.

2 Cut materials required for upholstering chair arms include 2" foam topper (glued to plywood arm rest) strip of self-welting and top and side panels of fabric.

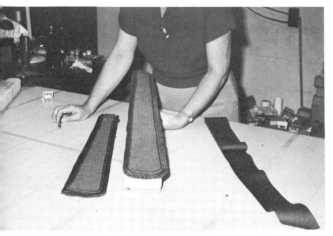

3 Welting is first stitched along edges of top and bottom panels. Side panels strip is then stitched to exposed flap.

4 To assure neat and snug fit, excess material is removed from inside seams of welting.

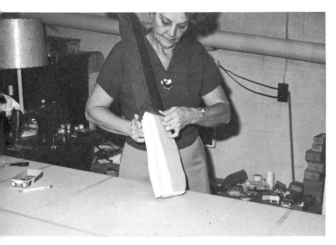

5 Cover is reversed, with welting bead exposed, and drawn like a stocking over foam and plywood. Cardboard strips relieve friction.

6 End flap, at bottom, is hand stitched to complete closure. All welted seams should be adjusted for snug alignment.

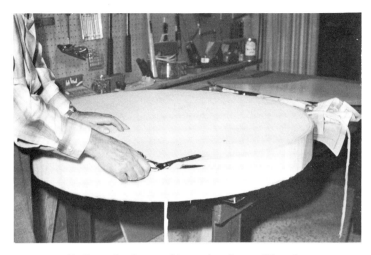

1 For circular cushion, the foam filler is cut to shape as illustrated on page 156. Scissors are used to snip ¼″ chamfer along edges.

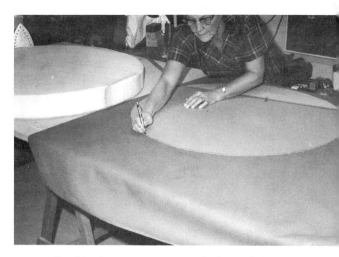

2 Circular pattern is marked on fabric. Material is cut only slightly oversize to provide snug fit over foam.

3 Fabric is folded to permit duplicate cutting of top and bottom panels in one operation.

4 Self-welting is attached, following stitching procedures pictured on page 157. One side is tried on, to check snug fit.

5 Section of one welted seam is left open for insertion of foam filler. Cover is then adjusted for snug and well-tailored fit.

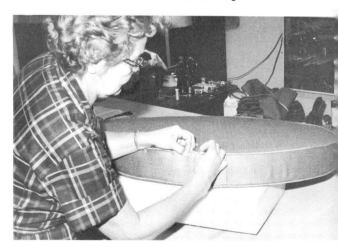

6 Opening in welted seam is then closed with hand stitching. Stretch quality of "Cohama" covering contributed to this fine workmanship.

HOW TO MAKE AND UPHOLSTER A TODDLER'S TUFFET

Nothing pleases toddlers more than to have their own very special portable perch for TV and similar sit-downs. You can make one in short order with left-over materials, by following the few simple steps of construction and upholstering pictured on these pages.

The top is made of a 12″ disk of ½″ plywood. Two pieces of scrapwood measuring 1″ x 3″ x 14″ make the crosslap base. Cutting and stitching of the cover follows the same procedures pictured on previous pages.

1 Plywood disk, measuring ½″ x 12″ is compass marked and cut with coping saw.

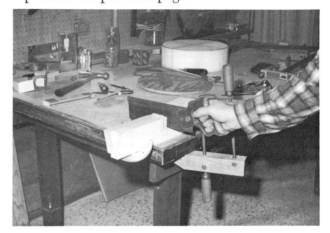

2 Reciprocating notches for crosslap cutouts of base are sawed simultaneously on two pieces.

3 Ends of base pieces are sawed on 1″ bevel slant and rounded off at corners with file or shaping tool.

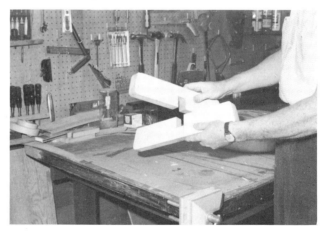

4 Finished base is fitted together with center cross-laps. All exposed edges are rounded.

5 Circular shape is marked from plywood disk on 4″ foam. Remnants of foam were used here.

6 Coping saw cuts circular shape of foam top.

7 Top edge of foam is chamfered and filler is glued to plywood disk.

8 Cover is made like those pictured on previous pages. But bottom, margin of material flaps over to be tacked to bottom surface of plywood.

9 Screws, counterbored from bottom, fasten base to plywood disk.

FIBERFILL CUSHIONS

While the upholstering of contemporary furniture usually adheres to the "tailored look" of flat foam cushions, some designs may require a soft, pillow-type cushion with crowned surfaces and fully rounded edges. Following the same covering procedures, already described, the filling for such cushions can be made of a urethane foam core, wrapped in Du Pont "Fiberfill."

As pictured on this page, the wrapping of Fiberfill batting over a foam core provides a layer of downy softness. And the plump cushion, thus produced, retains its shape under pressure of the resilient foam core.

Du Pont Fiberfill can be purchased at upholstery shops and some department stores. As illustrated here, it is extremely easy to apply and produces durable cushions which will not sag or bunch.

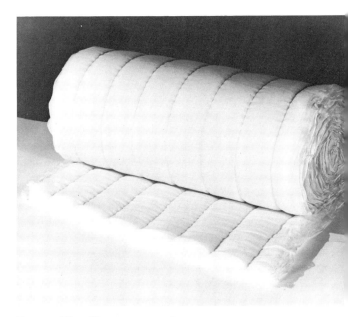

Dacron Fiberfill comes in rolls ranging in widths from 19″ to 62″.

Edges of batting are sewn around the foam core.

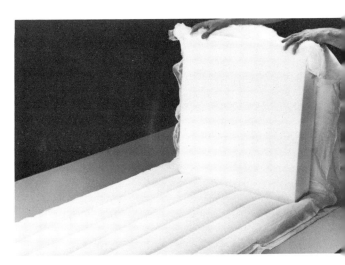

Urethane foam is wrapped in Fiberfill batting.

To assure snug fit, cushion cover is tailored slightly smaller than outside dimensions of filler.

Photos courtesy E. I. du Pont de Nemours & Co.

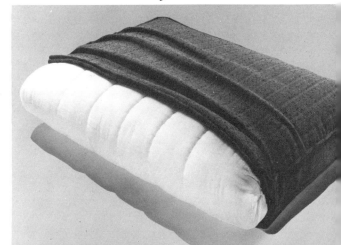

174

9

CONTEMPORARY FINISHING

Brushes of assorted sizes are the first requisite of a good finishing job. *Photo courtesy Tip Top Brush* Co.

CONTEMPORARY FINISHING

There are many methods of finishing contemporary furniture. It can be stained and painted or simply oiled or treated with clear agents to bring out the natural color and grain values of the wood.

Conventional finishes involving application and rubbing of successive top coats, to produce a high surface luster, have taken second place to natural finishes which penetrate into the wood rather than building up over it. Today's aim is to treat the wood in such a way that its natural features are brought out.

Furniture finished conventionally, with a build-up of coatings, has two surfaces:—the natural wood surface showing through a transparent coating and the coating *itself* which forms a hard and lustrous covering. The contemporary school contends the second surface is superfluous. Rather, they recommend that the finish penetrate into the wood and bring out its natural characteristics. This objective is

made possible by the oil and plastic coatings which are now available.

But while woods such as teak and walnut are ideally suited for natural, penetrating finishes, other woods are not. These are the woods which do not possess distinguished color or graining. They must be stained to a desired tone and must then be surface sealed with conventional clear coatings to enliven their adopted color.

Also for much contemporary construction, where fir plywood or miscellaneous types of lumber are employed, paint is used to subdue the wood and conceal its construction. The term "paint" is used here to denote the various types of enamels, plastics and other pigmented coatings which may be purchased for this purpose.

Finishing Materials and Equipment

As in all other operations, successful wood finishing requires proper finishing tools. A good selection of brushes, varied in size and type to the work being undertaken, will facilitate the job. As well as brushes, sandpaper of fine and medium grades, torn in quarter-sheet sizes, should be at hand. Lint-free rags, for rubbing

Hand block is used for preparatory sanding and for rubbing with fine abrasive paper between finishing coats. *Photo courtesy Pittsburgh Plate Glass* Co.

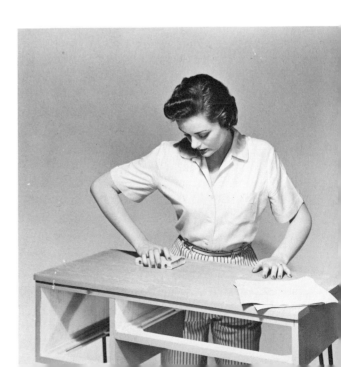

and cleaning, are a constant necessity. Fine steel wool will also be needed.

If much furniture finishing is to be done, spraying equipment, such as that illustrated on page 182, will hasten your operations and give a professional touch to your work. More elaborate sprayers, equipped with compression tanks, are used professionally. But the electric sprayer does a good job if used according to manufacturer's instructions.

One of the pitfalls of amateur wood finishing is the tendency of the uninitiated to get too preoccupied with the mechanics of their work. Thus in the process of brushing, sanding and rubbing they may damage clothing or furnishings which come in contact with their operations.

Keep in mind that finishing is not a clean business, and pick a location to do it where spillage from cans or daubs of oil and paint cannot inflict lasting damage. Protect all adjoining areas of the place where you are working with newspapers or drop cloths. And if you are applying slow-drying finishes, select a room that is relatively free of dust; otherwise your work will become peppered with dust specks during the drying period.

Small dents & depressions are "lifted" with wet blotting paper & hot iron.

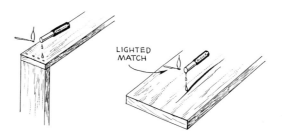

Stick shellac may be used to fill nail depressions & cracks.

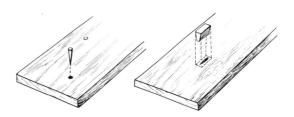

Pegs & wedges are used to repair small holes & damaged areas.

Paints are brushed on evenly in dust-free workroom. *Photo courtesy Pittsburgh Plate Glass Co.*

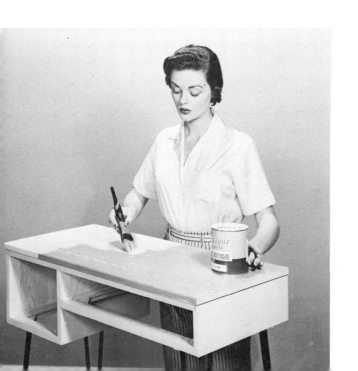

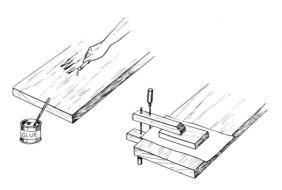

"Grain splinters" should be carefully glued and clamped.

Sanding is performed with the grain.

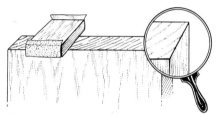

Sanding end grain. *NOTE:* Fine sandpaper produces interesting graining.

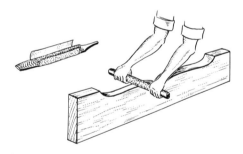

Spindle or file, wrapped in sandpaper is used for curved work.

Sandpaper is held loosely for dulling edges.

Preparing the Work for Finishing

Before any of the finishing steps are undertaken, the work should be carefully examined for scratches, mars, grain irregularities, dents, glue spots, and other imperfections.

Glue which has adhered at places of joining will not absorb stain and must, therefore, be carefully removed before any further steps are taken. Ordinarily, glue can be scraped or peeled off with a sharp knife, chisel, or cabinet scraper.

Dents and depressions may often be lifted by placing a wet piece of blotting paper directly over the spot and pressing it with a hot flatiron. Cracks, unless they are large ones, can ordinarily be filled with wood filler, toned to the same color as the desired final finish. Stick shellac, wood putty and plastic fillers may be bought in colors which blend exactly with most standard tones of finished wood. These are used to fill larger cracks or openings. All other imperfections will generally be overcome by the final and thorough use of sandpaper.

Too much emphasis cannot be placed on the importance of thorough sanding. Much of the basic sanding should be taken care of even before the work has been put together. The parts are easier to get at in this way. Two grades of sandpaper should be used; first a medium grade and then, for final sanding, a fine grade.

All sanding should be performed with the grain of the wood. To insure an even and thorough job a sandpaper block should be used wherever possible.

Natural Finishes

Linseed Oil Finish

For bringing out the inherent characteristics of wood, for the beautification of fine graining, and for the development of a lovely natural luster, no type of finish can surpass that which is obtained with boiled linseed oil. The luxurious, rich tones which oil produces in natural walnut, gumwood, teak, mahogany, and similar hardwoods causes this type of finish to be espe-

1 Prior to finishing, all parts are thoroughly sanded; electric sander facilitates job.

2 For final smoothing use fine sandpaper with hand block. Work with the grain.

3 Dust all parts carefully before applying finish.

4 Oil is first applied to center areas brushing toward edges and ends.

5 As brushing of oil progresses toward ends, watch for "dry-out" of absorbent areas and retouch.

6 Within period of one-half hour, rub off excess oil. Polish is obtained after second coat.

Stain is applied evenly from center area.

Soft cloth is used to rub stain, with the grain.

STEEL WOOL

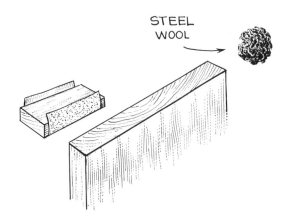

Fine sandpaper or steel wool is used to "brighten" end grain.

cially desirable. Moreover, the surface which is treated with oil is amply protected against ordinary damage, and it may be freshened up at any time with new applications of oil.

To produce this finish, it is first necessary to thin the boiled linseed oil with an equal quantity of turpentine. Add two tablespoons of vinegar to the pint. This mixture is applied with a brush, excess oil being removed with an absorbent rag. Successive coats of oil are applied, up to three or four, allowing each coat to dry before applying the next. The final coat is carefully rubbed with a clean cloth until a warm luster has been produced. The oil penetrates the wood, and once it has hardened, there is little likelihood of its coming off and soiling covers or clothing.

Danish Oil Finish

An excellent product, called Watco Danish Oil Finish performs wonders in the natural finishing of contemporary furniture. It is particularly effective for finishing such woods as teak and walnut where it penetrates to enrich the tone and surface graining. Moreover, because of a special ingredient, successive coats act as a sealant to fill the slight porosity of these woods and thus produce a soft, lustrous surface.

As illustrated in the accompanying photo-sequence, Watco is extremely simple to apply. It merely involves brushing on the oil, letting it penetrate into the wood, and then rubbing off the excess with a soft rag. The beauty of this finish is that it can always be refreshed with another application.

Stained Finishes

There are many different types of stain and each type has its own appeal. Many insist that the richer woods are better off without any stain, but most people do have occasion to use them.

Oil Stains

Oil stains are favored by many people because they are very easy to apply, and because they enable the worker to develop many interesting effects of tone and color, which would be difficult to attain with stains of other types. The oil stain is mixed from aniline colors compounded in oil and turpentine. Sometimes a small amount of linseed oil is added to give additional body to the stain. Stains of this type which are sold already mixed may contain benzol, benzine, or naphtha as their mixing ingredient.

The oil stain is a common favorite because it does not dry quickly and may be worked over with a rubbing rag after it has been applied. Moreover, it can be worked for tones and contrasts which cannot be obtained with any of the other varieties.

Stain Matching

A new stain matching system, called Weldwood Color Tones, makes it possible to mix over one hundred separate wood tones to match any desired shade. The stain is made of colorants which come in plastic pods to be mixed with two bases—light and dark. To obtain the exact stain tone, it is merely necessary to refer to dealers' color chip samples which show the various tones and specify the required mixture of colorant and base to produce each shade.

This new stain system differs from other pigmented wiping stains because penetration is controlled by a formula which ensures uniform effects on both soft and hard woods.

Blond Finishes

When light woods are used, a blond finish can be obtained simply by brushing a clear agent over the well sanded wood. But where exact tones are desired—or, where coloration of the light woods is mismatched—it may be well to apply a light stain.

For woods such as white oak, maple, birch,

Color tone stains are mixed to match over one-hundred selected tones.

Matched stains are brushed evenly on the wood and allowed a few moments to penetrate.

Excess stain is then rubbed off with a soft rag to bring out natural wood graining.

Photos courtesy U.S. Plywood Corporation

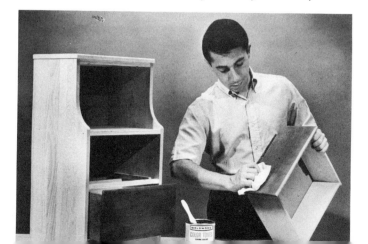

and spruce, a mixture of white paint, thinned fifty per cent with turpentine makes a suitable "blond" stain. It is worked like regular stains, being first brushed on and then rubbed off with a rag to bring out the natural wood graining.

If you want a tone other than off-white, make your stain of a mixture of light colored paints —grays, light greens, or light browns—to produce the exact desired shade.

Blond stains should be allowed to dry for twenty-four hours and should then be sealed in with a clear coating.

Clear Finishes

Plastic Coating

For contemporary furniture, where emphasis is placed on bringing out the natural qualities of the wood itself, thus avoiding the shine of conventional finishes, plastic top coatings are most appropriate. These produce a dull luster which seems to emanate from the wood. They apply closely to the wood and do not require the usual build-up and polishing of several successive coats.

One of the best of the plastics is produced by the Georgia-Pacific Corporation and is simply labeled "Plastic Top Coat." This can be applied with a brush. It flows on evenly and a single coat will do the job. Two coats are recommended, however, with light steel-wooling of the first.

Plastic top coat produces a soft, dull-luster finish that requires no further rubbing or polishing. Furthermore this is a durable finish which will withstand much abuse. It is easily wiped clean and can be waxed for added luster, if desired.

Shellac Finish

Before proceeding with any of the steps of shellacking, be sure that the article to be covered is thoroughly dry and clean, and that no dust or dirt is adhering to the surfaces.

For the first coat, the regular commercial

Spray finishes, in cans, are handy for small projects or for "touch-up" of finished parts. *Photo courtesy Pittsburgh Plate Glass Co.*

Spraying equipment can be used to advantage for finishing most projects. Skillful spraying produces professional results. *Photo courtesy Burgess Vibrocrafters, Inc.*

Paint rollers save time when finishing large areas. They can be used to advantage for painting full-size panels. *Photo courtesy Pittsburgh Plate Glass Co.*

1 Chiavari chair with finishing materials, ready for staining and finishing.

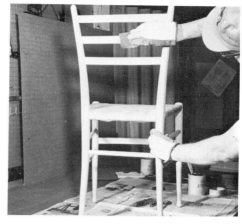

2 All parts are thoroughly sanded with fine sandpaper.

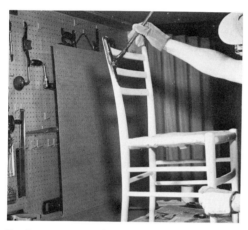

3 Stain is started at the top and brushed along one part at a time.

4 Excess stain is removed with rag from each part.

5 After stain becomes thoroughly dry, plastic coating is brushed on.

6 Between coats, after drying period, fine steel wool is used to polish all parts.

shellac should be cut with alcohol. It should be almost water thin. As shellac dries quickly when it is being applied, proceed briskly and evenly, working with the grain of the wood to avoid excessive brushing. The first thin coat is absorbed into the wood and provides a base for further coats.

After each coat of shellac, the work should be carefully rubbed with fine garnet paper (wet or dry) or steel wool. Ordinarily, three or four coats of shellac will provide an excellent finish. The final coat may be sprinkled with fine pumice stone and rubbed with an oil-soaked felt pad to obtain perfect smoothness. Afterward the work should be thoroughly waxed, both to protect the finish and to produce the proper luster.

Varnish Finish

One of the first requisites in varnishing is to find a dust-free workroom. The very fact that varnish dries slowly makes it vulnerable to any dust or dirt which may come in contact with it during the drying period.

However, after the varnish has been suitably cut with turpentine, the worker will delight in the fine free fashion in which it flows from the brush. Of course, in thin consistency, it can also be sprayed.

Although there are a number of quick-drying varnishes on the market, and while most of these are excellent, at least twelve hours should be allowed for each coat of varnish to become thoroughly dry. Each coat is carefully rubbed and smoothed with fine garnet paper before the next coat is applied. This provides an even binding surface for the succeeding coat.

Three good coats of varnish generally suffice. The final coat, which should be rubbed to a smooth luster, is polished thoroughly with a mixture of fine pumice stone and rottenstone.

Lacquer Finish

Lacquer provides an exceptionally durable finish. It does not crack or mar very readily and it resists the action of liquids, as well as changing climatic conditions. Moreover, it dries quickly and with the proper equipment it is not difficult to apply. These virtues also obtain for a variety of other plastic finishes.

Although lacquer may be purchased in various shades and colors, we are concerned at present with its use in clear form, that is, like shellac and varnish.

Because it is extremely quick in drying, the most satisfactory way of applying lacquer is with a sprayer. When skillfully sprayed on the work it dries uniformly and evenly. However, if it is properly diluted with lacquer thinner it may be brushed on, providing, of course, that the worker proceeds with due caution and takes care not to repeat brush strokes.

How to Paint

The same basic rules carry through in painting that apply in preparing work for a natural finish. However, painting is not quite as precise an operation as shellacking or varnishing. In most cases, paint will serve to conceal many of the blemishes which might mar or damage the appearance of work which is finished naturally. But it is a good idea to prepare the surface on which paint is to be applied.

Surfaces should be well sanded and free of grease spots, dirt, cracks, or nail holes. Nail holes and cracks can be filled with putty or similar filling substance. Porous, open-grained woods should be carefully filled.

It is always wise to give plywood a clear priming coat before proceeding with additional coats of paint. The priming coat is absorbed by the wood and provides a base for the coats which follow. Where several successive coats are to be applied, each coat, in turn, should be lightly sanded. The final coat is then evenly applied and permitted to remain unsanded.

One or more priming coats should also be applied as a base for enamel. At least two coats of enamel should be used.

10

CONTEMPORARY SOURCES

CONTEMPORARY FURNITURE
MANUFACTURERS AND SALES SOURCES

(A select list of American and European Sources)

American:

Bassett Furniture
Bassett, Virginia 24055

Brown Jordan
El Monte, Cal. 91734

Brown-Saltman
15000 S. Figueroa
Gardena, California

Design Import
511 E. Wells
Milwaukee, Wisc. 53202

Directional Furniture
979 Third Ave.
D & D Building
New York, N.Y.

Door Store
210 East 51st St.
New York, N.Y. 10022

Drexel Furniture Co.
Drexel, North Carolina

Dunbar Furniture Corp.
305 E. 63rd St.
New York, N.Y.

Founders Furniture
Box 339
Thomasville, N. C. 27360

Genada Imports
Box 204
Teaneck, N. J. 07666

Hammary Furniture
Lenoir, N. C. 28645

Harvey Probber, Inc.
155 E. 56th St.
New York, N.Y. 10022

Herman Miller, Inc.
Zeeland, Mich. 49464

Hendredon Furniture Co.
Morganton, N. C. 18655

Hunt Galleries, Inc.
2920 N. Center St.
Hickory, N. C. 28601

Knoll International, Inc.
320 Park Avenue
New York, N.Y.

Kroehler Manufacturing Co.
666 Lake Shore Drive
Chicago, Ill. 60611

Lane Company, Inc.
Altavista, Va. 24517

Marion Travis
Box 292
Statesville, N. C. 28677

Royal Systems
c/o Harold J. Siesel Co. Inc.
845 Third Avenue
New York, N.Y. 10022

Selig Manufacturing Co.
Leominster, Mass.

The Workbench
470 Park Ave., at 32nd St.
New York, N.Y. 10016

Tomlinson Furniture
High Point, N. C. 27261

Tri-Mark Designs
1006 Arch St.
Philadelphia, Pa. 19107

Weiman Furniture
Ramiseur, N. C. 27316

Wood-Made Cabinetry
Kreamer
Snyder County, Pa. 17833

European:

Alfred Senn
Meisenstrasse 9
4104 Oberwil
Switzerland

Artek
Keskuskatu 3
Helsinki, Finland

Artfort-Mobel Gmbh, Kolner
Strabe 256, 505 Perz-Westhofen
Postbox 1179
Maastricht/Holland

Bejra Mobler i Tibre Ab
543 Ol Tibro
Sweden

Carl Hansen & Son
97 Kochsgade
Odense, Denmark

C. M. Madsens Fabriker A/S
Haarby-Fyn
Denmark

Collins & Hayes Ltd.
Pauntley St.
London, N. 19
England

Desmond Ryan
Acorns
Gersewood Rd.
Hartley N. Dartford
Kent, England

Dux International Mobel AB
S-23100 Trellberg
Sweden

E. Kold Christenson A/S
Ole Nielsens Vej 33
Copenhagen, Denmark

Interna
10, Sankt Annae Plads
Copenhagen K Denmark
Byen 127 Giro 115502

Luigi Colombo Mobili
1-22063 Cantu (Como)
Via Milano 9
Italy

Mobelfabrik Erwin Behr
Wendelingen am Neckar 7317
West Germany

Mobili Imbottiti Bonacina
1-20036 Meda (Milano)
Viale Brianza 16, Italy

Oy Skanno Ab
Aleksanterink 38
Helsinki, Finland

Progressa AG
3414 Oberburg
Switzerland

A/S Ry Mobler
Skanderborgvej Ry St
Tif. Ry (0684) 192
Denmark

Salesco A/S
Rygaards Alle 131
Copenhagen-Hellerup
Denmark

S. M. Wincrantz Ab
Box 9252
S-54102
Skovde 2, Sweden

Wilhelm Renz KG
D-7030 Boblingen
Postfache 35
Germany

SOURCES OF RELATED MATERIALS, HARDWARE, KITS AND ACCESSORIES

Most of the related materials, hardware and accessories shown in this book may be found at your neighborhood building supply dealer as well as general hardware stores, lumberyards, do-it-yourself stores and diversified department stores. Such national chain organizations as *Grants, J. C. Penny, Montgomery-Ward, Sears, Woolworths,* and numerous others, offer a wide assortment of do-it-yourself materials and accessories, both in their stores and, more comprehensively, in their catalogs.

Some of the hard-to-find items can be ordered from catalogs of such specialized organizations as:

Albert Constantine & Sons, Inc.
2059 Eastchester Road
Bronx, N.Y. 10461

Barap Specialties
407 S. Monroe
Sturgis, Michigan 49091

Craftsman Wood Service Co.
2729 S. Mary Street
Chicago, Ill. 60608

The Hardware Emporium
353 Main Street
Danbury, Conn. 06810

Minnesota Woodworkers Supply Co.
925 Winnetka Ave., North
Minneapolis, Minn. 55427

All other materials and accessories, classified under the following headings, may be obtained by writing to the companies listed below. Some of these offer instructive literature on their products.

Adhesives:

Borden Adhesives
Box 266
Medina, Ohio 44256

Franklin Glue Co.
2020 Bruck St.
Columbus, Ohio 43207

3M Company
135 West 50th St.
New York, N.Y. 10020

Weldwood Packaged Products
Champion International
Kalamazoo, Mich. 49003

Aluminum Extrusions:

Macklanburg-Duncan Co.
Oklahoma City
Oklahoma 73125

Reynolds Metals Co.
Reynolds Metals Building
Richmond, Virginia

Attachable Legs & Pedestals:

Gerber Wrought Iron Products, Inc.
1510 Fairview Ave.
St. Louis, Missouri 63132

The Door Store
210 East 51st St.
New York, N.Y.

Furniture Kits:

Designer Kits (Metal)
39-06 Crescent St.
Long Island City, N.Y. 11101

Doo-It Store
1038 North Woodward
Royal Oak, Michigan

Door Store
3140 M Street N. W.
Washington, D.C. 20007

Furn-a-Kit
140 East Union Ave.
East Rutherford, N. J. 07073

Peninsula Wood Products
Box 22
Sturgeon Bay, Wisconsin 54235

Glass:

American Saint Gobain Corp.
c/o Turner & Feeney, Inc.
444 Madison Ave.
New York, N.Y.

PPG Industries, Inc.
One-Gateway Center
Pittsburgh, Pennsylvania 15222

Libby-Owens-Ford Glass Co.
811 Madison Ave.
Toledo, Ohio

Hardware—General:

The Stanley Works
New Britain, Conn. 06050

Paints—Stains—Finishes:

Deft
812 Maple Ave.
Torrance, Cal. 90503

E. I. DuPont de Nemours & Co.
Wilmington, Deleware

Pittsburgh Plate Glass Co.
632 Fort Duquesne Blvd.
Pittsburgh, Pennsylvania

Pratt & Lambert, Inc.
75 Tonowanda St.
Buffalo, N.Y.

Watco-Dennis Corp.
"Watco" Danish Oil Finish
1756 22nd St.
Santa Monica, Cal. 90404

Plywood:

American Plywood Association
Tacoma, Wash. 98401

Hardwood Plywood Manufacturers Association
2300 S. Walter Reed Drive
P. O. Box 6246
Shirlington Station
Arlington, Virginia 22206

Shelf Brackets & Standards:

Ardor Manufacturing Co.
1038 N. Woodward
Royal Oak, Mich. 48067

Door Store
3140 M St., N. W.
Washington, D. C. 20007

Knape & Vogt Manufacturing Co.
Grand Rapids, Michigan

The Stanley Works
New Britain, Conn. 06050

Surfacing Materials & Veneers:

Armstrong Cork Co.
Lancaster, Pennsylvania

Carr Adhesive Products, Inc.
14201 Industrial Ave., South
Cleveland, Ohio 44137

Comark Plastic Division
Con-Tact
1407 Broadway
New York, N.Y. 10018

Homecraft Veneer
Box 3
Latrobe, Pa. 15650

General Tire & Rubber Co.
P. O. Box 951
Akron, Ohio 44329

Morgan Adhesives Co.
MACtac Products
4500 Darrow Road
Stow, Ohio 44224

3-M Company
135 W. 50th St.
New York, N.Y. 10020

U. S. Plywood-Champion Papers, Inc.
Box 61
New York, N.Y. 10046

U. S. Rubber Co.
Coated Fabrics & Koylon Dept.
Mishawaka, Indiana

Upholstering Materials:

Acushnet Process Co.
Belville Ave.
New Bedford, Mass.

General Foam Corp.
640 W. 134th St.
New York, N.Y.

Firestone Tire & Rubber Co.
Fall River, Mass.

BIBLIOGRAPHY

BAUHAUS AND BAUHAUS PEOPLE, ed. by Eckard Neumann; pub. by Van Nostrand Reinhold, N.Y.

CONTEMPORARY FURNITURE, by Alexander F. Bick; pub. by Bruce Publishing Co., Milwaukee, Wisc.

DECORATIVE ART IN MODERN INTERIORS, by Ella Moody; pub. by Viking Press, N.Y.

DESIGNER FURNITURE ANYONE CAN MAKE, by William E. Schremp; pub. by Simon & Schuster, N.Y.

MAKING MODERN DANISH FURNITURE, by Rolf Schutze; pub. by Van Nostrand Reinhold, N.Y.

MODERN FURNITURE, by Ella Moody; pub. by Dutton, N.Y.

MODERN FURNITURE AND DECORATION, by Robert Harling; pub. by Viking Press, N.Y.

MODERN SCANDINAVIAN FURNITURE, by Ulf Hard Segerstad; pub. by Bedminster Press, Totowa, N. J.

NEW DESIGN IN WOOD, by Donald J. Willcox; pub. by Van Nostrand Reinhold, N.Y.

NEW FURNITURE (Vols. 8, 9 & 10) ed. by Gerd Hatje & Karl Kaspar; pub. by Praeger, N.Y.

ORGANIC DESIGN IN HOME FURNISHINGS, by Elliot F. Noyes; pub. by Museum of Modern Art, N.Y.

index